BASICS

ARCHITECTURE

02

Construction + Materiality

Lorraine Farrelly

ava | Academia
the environment of learning

An AVA Book

Published by AVA Publishing SA
Rue des Fontenailles 16
Case Postale
1000 Lausanne 6
Switzerland
Telephone: +41 786 005 109
Email: enquiries@avabooks.ch

Distributed by Thames & Hudson
(ex-North America)
181a High Holborn
London WC1V 7QX
United Kingdom
Telephone: +44 20 7845 5000
Fax: +44 20 7845 5055
Email: sales@thameshudson.co.uk
www.thamesandhudson.com

Distributed in the USA & Canada by:
Ingram Publisher Services Inc.
1 Ingram Blvd.
La Vergne, TN 37086
USA
Telephone: +1 866 400 5351
Fax: +1 800 838 1149
Email: customer.service@ingrampublisherservices.com

English Language Support Office
AVA Publishing (UK) Ltd.
Telephone: +44 1903 204 455
Email: enquiries@avabooks.ch

ISBN 978-2-940373-83-3
and 2-940373-83-3

10 9 8 7 6 5 4 3 2 1

Design by Jane Harper

Production by AVA
Book Production Pte Ltd, Singapore
Telephone: +65 6334 8173
Fax: +65 6259 9830
Email: production@avabooks.com.sg

Project: The Liquorish Bar
Location: London, UK
Architects: Nissen Adams
Date: 2006

The door of this venue is made
from reclaimed timbers, which are
set in a stainless steel frame. The
surrounding wall is made from cast
concrete and the building's number
(123) has been set directly into the
concrete façade.

Contents

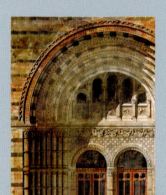

Construction + materiality

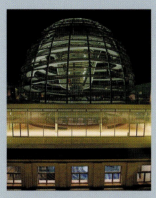

Contents

Materials create an ambience and provide texture or substance to architecture. To understand how to use materials effectively, a designer needs to have an understanding of precedent or how materials have been used historically and an awareness of innovations in material application. Both can provide a useful way to develop a range of design approaches.

Construction + Materiality introduces the ideas that 'make' architecture and the materials used to create and define spaces. The structure (or frame) that supports a building can be considered to be analogous to the skeleton of a body, and the materials that the structure holds in place akin to the tissue and skin that define a body's shape and specificity. In this way, construction techniques and materials are the starting point for architectural design; they create the possibilities for shape, form and space.

For an architect to use materials effectively, a sound understanding of construction methods and practices is essential. Construction methods and materials can be expressed in such a way that they immediately reveal the architectural idea behind a building. But not all architecture is 'true' and the idea of 'truth to materials' is an essential consideration when understanding architecture.

In architectural terms, to be 'true' is to be honest. A building that uses brick to construct a wall, which in turn supports a roof, is using materials honestly. A steel-framed building that incorporates a brick wall is not necessarily true to its materials because there is a sense of 'hiding' the building's real structure and creating an illusion of another sort of architecture. A building's structure does not always have to be obviously revealed: sometimes an architect may want to create a sense of illusion as part of his or her design idea (for example, to make a heavy material appear light by introducing a steel beam), but to make a concrete or steel framed building appear like a brick building conflicts with the idea of 'truth' to materials.

In addition to the concept of architectural 'truth', some materials are strongly connected to their place or origin. Stone, for example, belongs to the ground where it is found or quarried. Similarly, timber is a resource that is part of a natural landscape. Other materials, such as concrete and glass, are much less connected to the identity of a location

Project: Leslie L Dan Pharmacy Building, University of Toronto
Location: Toronto, Canada
Architects: Foster + Partners with Moffat Kinoshita Architects
Dates: 2002–2006

This building has been carefully designed to sensitively respond to its immediate surroundings. Its main mass is elevated above a 20-metre, five-storey, colonnaded circulation space. Two coloured pods are suspended within this space, the larger of which houses a 60-seat lecture theatre and a reading room, with the other housing a smaller classroom and the faculty lounge.

Construction + materiality

or specific place. Instead, they are part of an industry that manufactures materials, using raw ingredients that can belong and be made anywhere.

Increasingly, contemporary designers are taking materials from different contexts and environments and applying them inventively in architecture. Materials from the world of product, fashion and furniture design are being considered for interior and exterior architectural applications. The standard convention of using traditional materials for building is changing as issues of cost and sustainability become ever more important. Thinking carefully about which materials to source and specify, how far they have travelled and whether they can be recycled or reused is the responsibility of the architect when designing a building or space.

An architect needs to understand the nature of materials and their possibilities and limitations before they can be used to create buildings and spaces. This book introduces traditional, manufactured and more contemporary materials. Each chapter describes a particular material (or materials) in terms of its historical development and in the context of its application. This is accompanied by a canon of work from a 'grand master' who has championed the development of an architecture associated with the material. Practical case studies from a range of contemporary architects will demonstrate the innovative use of materials at various scales. The final chapter of the book explores issues of sustainability, innovation and the future of materials and construction techniques.

As an architect, understanding the changing nature of materials is critical. To be aware of the range and properties of the materials at your disposal is to extend the possibility of your design potential.

'Let every material be true to itself... brick should appear as brick, wood as wood, iron as iron, each according to its own statistical laws.'
Gottfried Semper

Construction + materiality

Brick and stone

Stone is found or excavated from the ground and brick is moulded from the earth. These materials have weight and solidity that belongs to a place. This chapter looks at the use of stone and brick in architecture and explores their natural colour, texture and surface.

Concrete

Concrete has the potential to be moulded and shaped to create dynamic form and, with reinforcement, can span enormous distances and achieve great heights. This chapter explores the view that concrete is *the* flexible material of the twenty-first century.

Timber

This chapter explores the many architectural possibilities that timber offers. There are many ways to apply timber because it is easily worked, its aesthetic variable depending on the nature of the wood's grain.

Glass and steel

Individually these materials are used in a range of different design contexts. In architecture, they allow a space to be light and a structure to be elegant. This chapter highlights the ways in which steel and glass have the potential to create an architecture that is both beautiful and subtly engineered.

Composite materials

These materials can be created and manufactured from a series of processes. The origin of a composite material may be natural but it can be further modified or engineered to create a material that has new possibilities, both structurally and in terms of its application.

Innovation, sustainability and the future

Manufacturing and technological advances present new possibilities for materials in architecture. This chapter looks at how these ideas suggest an exciting future for architecture.

This book introduces different aspects of construction and materiality in architecture via dedicated chapters for each topic. Each chapter provides examples of different construction techniques and materials at various stages of the architectural design process. The examples shown here are contributions from a range of contemporary architects and, together with detailed analysis in the text, form a book that offers a unique insight into the practical and professional world of architectural design.

Captions
Provide contextual information about each featured project and highlight the practical application of key principles.

Section headings
Each chapter unit has a clear heading to allow readers to quickly locate an area of interest.

Cultural and material context

48 | 49

Project: Chapel Notre Dame du Haut (right)
Location: Ronchamp, France
Architect: Le Corbusier
Date: 1954

Le Corbusier's Chapel Notre Dame du Haut at Ronchamp uses concrete to create a dramatic and sculptural form on both the exterior and interior spaces. The building is punctured with holes filled with coloured glass and these bring light into the chapel illuminating the interior space. The building appears as a sculptural element in the natural landscape.

Topography
Topography is concerned with local detail in general, including not only relief but also vegetative and human-made features, and even local history and culture. This meaning is less common in America, where topographic maps with elevation contours have made 'topography' synonymous with relief. The older sense of Topography as the study of place still has currency in Europe.

Unlike other construction materials, which may strongly connect with the place of their origin, concrete is made from ingredients that can now be mixed anywhere. This not only makes it flexible in terms of manufacture, but also does not restrict the material to a particular location. This affords concrete a sense of anonymity, which means it is much less limited by traditional ideas and concepts than other materials: it can be anything, anywhere. Notwithstanding this, the use of concrete in architecture is (usually) still informed by local ideas of construction, form, function and other aspects of context.

Concrete and the era of Modernism
The prominent Modernists of the early 20th century, notably Le Corbusier and Auguste Perret, exploited the flexibility of concrete to create new forms and shapes. They designed cities for the future that contained strong, bold and tall structures all made from concrete.

Title: Ciudad de las Artes y las Ciencias (facing page)
Location: Valencia, Spain
Architect: Santiago Calatrava
Date: 2001

The Ciudad de las Artes y las Ciencias is an urban cultural centre. It reacts to the local environment and uses white concrete to contrast with the blue Spanish skies. The concrete is used with local tile to connect the finish with traditional industries.

Continuing this tradition, Brazilian architect Oscar Niemeyer uses concrete in his designs to respond to organic forms in the landscape. Niemeyer extends the landscape and **topography** with his architectural ideas, producing dramatic shapes on rolling planes or landscapes that are made from carpets of concrete.

In South America, Luis Barragan introduced colour to his architecture to connect his building designs and materials with the traditional colours found in the landscape and culture of the region. Barragan's architecture has been described as similar to an abstract painting with wall surfaces coloured to contrast against one another and sharp coloured walls framing views across landscapes. His architecture is about the surface experience, walls that are rendered in cement and then painted, to create abstract planes.

Contemporary 21st century architecture uses concrete to create ever taller, more dramatic statements. Daniel Libeskind, for example, specified the use of concrete in his designs for Berlin's Jewish Museum to dramatise and accentuate the Jewish experience in wartime Germany, producing both a provocative and commemorative result (see page 40).

Concrete is the substance of our new buildings, our greatest edifices and our skyscrapers, and it will challenge the future of architectural forms. Yet even so, the adaptation of concrete to respond to local cultural and climatic issues is essential for its survival.

Information panels
Provide additional information about technical terms that are used in the body text.

Introductions
Each unit's introduction appears in bold text and outlines the concepts that are to be discussed.

Chapter navigation
Highlights the current chapter unit and lists the previous and following units.

Construction + materiality

Grand master pages
Focus on the work of an
architect who has championed
the use of a particular material.

Images
Examples from architects and
designers bring the principles
under discussion to life.

Timelines
Provide details of
significant projects
in an architect's
canon of work.

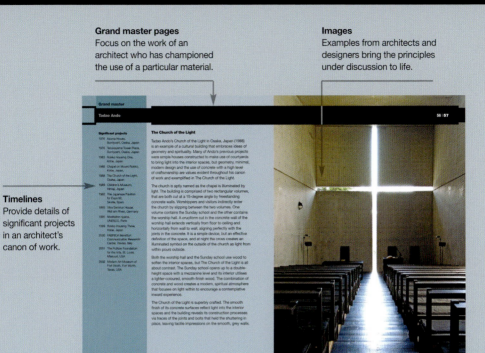

Significant projects

1974	Azuma House, Sumiyoshi, Osaka, Japan
1976	Tezukayama Tower Plaza, Sumiyoshi, Osaka, Japan
1983	Rokko Housing One, Kobe, Japan
1988	Chapel on Mount Rokko, Kobe, Japan
1989	The Church of the Light, Osaka, Japan
1989	Children's Museum, Himeji, Japan
1992	The Japanese Pavilion for Expo 92, Seville, Spain
1993	Vitra Seminar House, Weil am Rhein, Germany
1991	Meditation space, UNESCO, Paris
1999	Rokko Housing Three, Kobe, Japan
2000	FABRICA Benetton Communication Research Center, Treviso, Italy
2001	The Pulitzer Foundation for the Arts, St. Louis, Missouri, USA
2002	Modern Art Museum of Fort Worth, Fort Worth, Texas, USA

The Church of the Light

Tadao Ando's Church of the Light in Osaka, Japan (1989) is an example of a cultural building that embraces ideas of geometry and spirituality. Many of Ando's previous projects were simple houses constructed to make use of courtyards to bring light into the interior spaces, but geometry, minimal, modern design and the use of concrete with a high level of craftsmanship are values evident throughout his canon of work and exemplified in The Church of the Light.

The church is aptly named as the chapel is illuminated by light. The building is comprised of two rectangular volumes, that are both cut at a 15-degree angle by freestanding concrete walls. Worshippers and visitors indirectly enter the church by slipping between the two volumes. One volume contains the Sunday school and the other contains the worship hall. A cruciform cut in the concrete wall of the worship hall extends vertically from floor to ceiling and horizontally from wall to wall, aligning perfectly with the joints in the concrete. It is a simple device, but an effective definition of the space, and at night the cross creates an illuminated symbol on the outside of the church as light from within pours outside.

Both the worship hall and the Sunday school use wood to soften the interior spaces, but The Church of the Light is all about contrast. The Sunday school opens up to a double-height space with a mezzanine level and its interior utilises a lighter-coloured, smooth-finish wood. The combination of concrete and wood creates a modern, spiritual atmosphere that focuses on light within to encourage a contemplative inward experience.

The Church of the Light is superbly crafted. The smooth finish of its concrete surfaces reflect light into the interior spaces and the building reveals its construction processes via traces of the joints and bolts that held the shuttering in place, leaving tactile impressions on the smooth, grey walls.

An interior view of the worship hall

Concrete

Case study pages
Focus on a project or build
that demonstrates an
innovative use of materials.

Quotes
Provide key insight
from professional
architects.

Body text
In-depth
discussion of
working methods
and best practice
is covered in the
book's body copy.

'As architects, my colleagues and I had been engaged for many years in meeting the challenge of social, technological and lifestyle change, the way they interlock and looking at the re-evaluation of the workplace as a good place to be. This inspiration has permeated down into the building itself.'
Sir Norman Foster

The McLaren Technology Centre is the corporate and manufacturing headquarters for the McLaren Group. Designed by Foster + Partners, the group's state-of-the-art centre is located in Surrey, England. Foster + Partners are renowned internationally for their approach, which combines functional architectural design with an elegance in engineering. This combination produces expressive buildings that envelope and contain function, but challenge preconceptions of space via the innovative use of building materials.

The design brief
The McLaren headquarters fits the paradigm of a Foster + Partners building. McLaren depends on the continued development of high technology in order to produce some of the fastest Formula One cars in the world. The architecture that would become the company's headquarters needed to reflect this technological sophistication and serve as a 'laboratory' for McLaren's innovation.

McLaren came to the architects with a number of preconceptions, not about what the architecture should look like, but what the spirit of the building, its aspirations and its social generators should be.

The building's site plan shows the scheme within its context, surrounded by a lake and carefully organised planting

Foster + Partners were asked to ensure that the headquarters would house the majority of the McLaren Group's employees (who had been previously scattered across 18 locations in Surrey). The architects worked with the client to respond to their working methodology and processes to ensure that the building could accommodate their experimental, developmental and manufacturing needs.

There was a natural synergy between McLaren and Foster + Partners and in determining what the architect and client, both of whom came from very different design disciplines, wanted to achieve.

Glass and steel

An exterior view of the McLaren headquarters

Grand master: Ludwig Mies van der Rohe · The McLaren Technology Centre

How to get the most out of this book

The most basic of building materials are those that come from the ground, either found as part of the landscape (such as stone), or sourced from the earth (such as clay, which can then be moulded into bricks). Architecture built from such materials will literally become a part of its surrounding landscape. Other rocks or stones such as granite or marble (which are mined or quarried) can also be incorporated into designs to produce architecture that is strongly connected to its place of origin.

Perhaps surprisingly, stone is a versatile material. It can be used for a structure's ground surface, walls and roof (if carefully selected and cut); it can be shaped or sliced into thin slabs or heavy monolithic blocks, and its physical properties mean that it retains heat in the winter and remains cool in the summer. Additionally, there is a degree of symbolism associated with stone. It is often used for memorials or to mark a point in the landscape because it has a timeless, indestructible quality, which suggests a degree of permanence and solidity.

Stone and brick structures characteristically highlight their materials as key building components because they form a series of clearly visible pieces that belong to the bigger jigsaw of the architecture. There is a building protocol that is specifically associated with brick and stone architecture. For example, openings in stone walls need to be supported with lintels; and in brick walls, an arch is used to support material under compression.

Regardless of advances in construction technologies, stone or brick buildings will retain their sense of place within the context of the natural environment. Although it may have been shaped or adjusted by the mason or the craftsman, stone is nature's 'found' material and brick is the earth moulded – as such it is the closest that the architect can get to nature's grain.

Title: Entrance of the Natural History Museum
Location: London, UK
Architects: Alfred Waterhouse
Dates: 1830

Terracotta tiles were used on the interior and exterior walls of London's Natural History Museum, serving both decorative and practical functions. The museum's entrance is constructed from a range of different coloured bricks that have been laid using many different courses to highlight the 'horizontality' of the building. Decorative features, also constructed from tile and marble, serve to create a highly adorned and three-dimensional effect.

3100–2500 BC
Skara Brae, Scotland

This Neolithic village is located in Orkney (off the north coast of Scotland). It comprises a series of living spaces that are lined with stone and covered with earth. Within the living spaces there are shelves, seating areas and evidence of tables, all made from stone. Skara Brae is one of the earliest examples of a complete stone settlement.

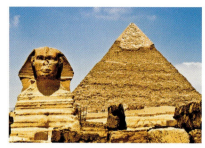

c.2560 BC
Great Pyramid of Giza, Egypt

Built by the Ancient Egyptians as tombs for their Pharaohs, the pyramids at Giza were constructed from huge limestone blocks that were brought to the site along the River Nile. A rough limestone was used for the main core of the pyramids and a finer, white limestone with a polished finish was used as the outer stone.

c.1530 BC
Hypostyle Hall, Egypt

The Hypostyle Hall is part of a complex of buildings situated in Karnak, near Luxor, Egypt. The complex comprises a number of temples built over a period of 1300 years. The Hypostyle Hall is an impressive 28-metre-high structure containing a series of papyrus columns made from sandstone, which would have originally supported a stone roof.

1420
Cupola (of the Basilica di Santa Maria del Fiore), Italy
Filippo Brunelleschi

Designed by Filippo Brunelleschi, the cupola of the Basilica di Santa Maria del Fiore in Florence, Italy, consists of a double-walled dome made of several million bricks, with large stones supporting the main structure. The base of the dome is held in tension with iron chains.

1514–1737
Hampton Court Palace, England
Various architects

Successive monarchs from the early 16th century have developed this palace. It comprises a series of houses, courtyards and surrounding formal gardens that were expanded to accommodate bishops (at first) and then royalty and their families and servants. The buildings are made of brick, with stone and brick structures added over successive generations.

1566–1571
Villa Rotunda, Italy
Andrea Palladio

Andrea Palladio's Villa Rotunda has a completely symmetrical plan and a circular hall roofed with a dome. This Renaissance-style building was made from stone and heavily influenced by Greek and Roman temples in terms of its materiality and proportion.

c.70–80
Coliseum, Italy

This amphitheatre was built as an arena for public spectacles and gladiator contests. The exterior was made of travertine stone and the interior areas were later built from brick. Originally, the building had wooden floors and temporary structures built within it.

1163–1250
Notre Dame de Paris, France
Maurice de Sully

Built on an island in the River Seine, Notre Dame de Paris is widely considered one of the finest examples of French Gothic architecture in the world. The cathedral has two towers at its front and also a distinctive rose window. It is built of cut stone and uses flying buttresses (a type of external framing system), to support the exterior walls.

c.1300
Piazza della Signoria, Italy

The Piazza della Signoria is an L-shaped square in front of the Palazzo Vecchio in Florence, Italy. The piazza originally had a surface made of ancient brick and the buildings that surround it are made of marble. This square has become an open-air museum with a range of statues and art works on display.

1859
Red House, England
Philip Webb

Philip Webb designed this house, which is located in Kent, England, for William Morris. Webb specified the use of local materials and craftsmen (as part of the arts and crafts tradition) to realise the building, which referenced a local style of architecture. The house is made from brick with arched openings and a clay-tiled roof.

1906–1910
Casa Mila, Spain
Antonio Gaudí

Constructed almost entirely from locally-sourced stone, Casa Mila was a residential building designed by Antonio Gaudí. The walls are sculpted in a distinctive, biomorphic fashion and suggest an almost wave-like form. The building's roof is also of note: its chimneys appear as abstract pieces of sculpture producing a surreal landscape on the Barcelona skyline.

1960
The Salk Institute, USA
Louis Kahn

Kahn used baked brick in the building of this Californian college campus. The campus contains a series of buildings for teaching and accommodation that have been constructed using traditional building techniques. The modernist complex consists of two symmetrical buildings with a stream of water flowing in the middle of a courtyard that separates the two.

Timeline: brick and stone › Origins and chronology

Some of the earliest settlements and architectural structures that survive are made of stone. The Skara Brae site in Orkney, Scotland, is Europe's most complete example of a Neolithic village; it dates back to around 3100 BC and consists of approximately ten stone-built dwellings. Found stone was lifted, stacked, sized and carved to create the walls, roof and even the furniture within the dwellings.

Brick

Traditionally, bricks were manufactured by placing mud in simple wooden frames and allowing these to 'bake' in the sun. In many countries this method of manufacture is still used. One of the earliest examples (c.7050 BC) of the use of such shaped bricks was found in a Neolithic settlement in southern Turkey. Kiln-fired bricks are believed to have arisen in the Middle East several thousand years later.

Fired bricks were further developed by the Romans to allow them to engineer structures such as aqueducts, which required arches to be built within the structure. As they are much more resistant to cold and moist weather conditions, fired bricks enabled the construction of permanent buildings in regions where harsher climates had precluded the use of mud bricks. Bricks have the added benefit of slowly storing heat energy from the sun during the day and continuing to release heat for several hours after sunset.

During the 15th and 17th centuries in much European architecture brick was usually covered by plaster. It was not until the late 18th century, with the start of the Industrial Revolution, that brick was once again used expressively in construction.

Modern architecture increasingly uses concrete- and steel-frame structures to achieve ever larger and taller buildings; however, brick remains a popular and frequently used material for small-scale buildings such as domestic houses.

Project: The Great Wall
Location: Shanhaiguan (east) to Lop Nur (west), China
Date: From the fifth century BC to the 16th century

The Great Wall was constructed over a vast geographical area and the materials used were locally sourced. Quarried limestone block was used in the areas of wall near Beijing; other sites saw quarried granite and fired brick used as key building materials. In particularly remote areas that had a lack of locally available materials, rammed earth was used for construction.

Brick and stone

Stone

The earliest stone structures were defensive structures.
Stone is solid, heavy and creates a sense of safety and
security. Structures such as the Great Wall of China (parts
of which date back to the fifth century BC) still remain as
powerful divisions in the landscape. In some areas, the Great
Wall was constructed using rammed earth that was dressed
in local stone. It was both practical (defining boundaries and
territories) and symbolic.

Monumentalism

Stone has long been associated with permanence and solidity. A stone building has a presence, which is why the material has been used to construct many of our symbolic and/or monumental cathedrals, castles and civic buildings. In Ancient Egypt the Great Pyramids of Giza (c.2560 BC) were constructed from layers of stone. Here, stone was used to create monumental structures that signified power, authority and longevity.

The Parthenon in Greece is one of the most significant structures in Europe. Built initially as a temple dedicated to Athena, it was later used as a Christian church and then a mosque. It now houses a museum detailing how the structure has adapted to its changing functions over the years. The Parthenon was built under the general supervision of the sculptor Phidias. Construction began in 447 BC, and the building was substantially completed by 432 BC, but work on the decorations continued until at least 431 BC. Some of the financial accounts for the Parthenon survive and show that the largest single expense was transporting the stone from Mount Pentelicus, about 16 kilometres from Athens, to the Acropolis.

One of the great advantages of stone buildings is that they have survived the ravages of time and allow us to learn from architects past. In Europe the most dramatic and impressive architecture is made of durable stone. Stone buildings today remain synonymous with an idea of permanence, quality and solidity, and this suggests a connection between the architectural past, present and the future.

Project: Parthenon
Location: Athens, Greece
Architects: Iktinos and Kallikrates
Date: c.447–432 BC

The Parthenon is an icon of classical architecture. The structure comprises a series of columns, beams and walls that are all made from locally sourced stone and marble. Each of the Parthenon's columns appear as if created from a single piece of stone, but they are actually constructed from a series of interlocking carved stone components that are held together with discreet iron clamps.

Brick and stone

Of all the materials available to the architect, it is arguably the use of stone and brick that produces an architecture most closely associated with its geographical and cultural context. One reason for this is that historically stone would have been sourced near the construction site; small quarries where the material was extracted out of the ground have been found near many Neolithic settlements, for example.

In their most basic form, structures can be created by carefully stacking stone pieces together in such a way that they complement one another and create an integrated mass (a dry stone wall is an example of this). More complex stone buildings use interlocking pieces that are carefully cut to create larger, more structurally efficient forms.

Initially, stone was used in construction in its raw state, but as stonemasonry skills developed the surface became an opportunity for architectural expression. For example, the stone columns that support the temple of the Erechtheion in Athens, Greece, have been carved to create a series of **caryatids**. Similarly, cathedrals and places of worship often have symbolic figures carved into the stone so that they appear as part of the wall or building.

As with stone, brick also belongs to its place of origin and manufacture. Both are sourced from the earth and create their own material landscape. Bricks were first made from clay or mud that was first shaped and then baked in the sun (see page 16), but with the introduction of kiln-firing, a manufactured, industrially processed material that was much more associated with utilitarian buildings, factories and houses was produced.

Bricks are easy to handle and laid using a modular system. As such, structures built from bricks can be assembled fairly swiftly and easily. However, this should not imply that brickwork produces 'plain' architecture as there is a language of expression when brick is used in buildings.

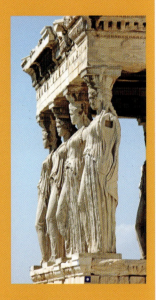

Caryatids

A caryatid is a sculpted female figure serving as an architectural support (instead of a column or pillar). The figure's head supports the building's entablature.

Some of the earliest known examples were found in the treasuries of Delphi, dating to about the sixth century BC. The best-known examples are the six figures of the Caryatid Porch of the Erechtheion on the Acropolis at Athens (pictured). One of those original six figures, removed by Lord Elgin in the early 1800s, is now in the British Museum in London. The other five figures are in the Acropolis Museum, and have been replaced onsite by replicas.

Both stone and bricks can be reused. Once extracted from the ground and cut, stone might be used to build a wall, but after time the wall could be dismantled and the cut stone could then be reused in another structure. Reclaimed bricks made in the Georgian or Victorian period are expensive materials to use in construction today: there is a softness to the texture of the material due to age and the process of manufacture is difficult to replicate using contemporary and mass manufacturing processes.

Title: Compton Verney House
Location: Warwickshire, UK
Architects: Stanton Williams Architects
Date: 1997

Stanton Williams Architects were commissioned to extend an existing stately home into an arts venue. The building is carefully detailed and uses stone in a considered and subtle way to reinvent the existing architecture. The new spaces work in harmony with the existing ones, creating a fluid architectural promenade through the building for visitors.

Project: High House
Location: Vaduz, Liechtenstein
Architect: Hansjörg Göritz
Date: 2008

High House was the first new
dedicated parliament building
for Liechtenstein. The scheme
comprises a main assembly and
a series of offices, all of which are
connected by a large open space.
The buildings collectively use around
one million bricks.

Both stone and brick can be used in a range of architectural applications. As both materials have load-bearing potential to support their own weight (and more) they are used most effectively in constructing walls and for floor surfaces.

Walls

A brick wall requires standard components. For example, a foundation or footing will provide stability, and when openings are created (for doors or windows), the bricks above the aperture will need to be supported. Traditionally an arch was used as a self-supporting method of framing an opening; nowadays lintels serve the same purpose. Lintels may be concrete or steel and they may be expressed or hidden. A hidden lintel sits within the cavity of a wall and the bricks appear to be suspended from it.

Both brick and stone walls were originally built to support the load or weight of their building. However, developments in material manufacture and technology have changed the way both materials are used. Solid, brick or stone load-bearing walls are slow to construct and require a great deal of expensive materials. Though less 'true', cladding can give the impression of solid brick and stone walls but offers the architect more flexibility in terms of time and money. Thin layers of stone or brick are attached to a steel or concrete frame providing a system that looks effective but uses less material and can be built more efficiently.

Rubble walls are traditionally built from found stones that are selected and organised so that they all complement one another. Usually larger stones create the base and smaller stones are used to fill gaps as the wall progresses – the higher the wall the smaller the stones used.

A gabion wall is usually constructed by filling a wire-framed mesh with found rocks. These have been used as engineering structures that easily withstand lateral forces, such as a retaining wall that may be used to hold back large areas of earth. Latterly gabion walls are being used in contemporary building schemes as a variable external finish according to the size and type of stone used.

Floors

Stone and brick can be used as a floor covering to great effect. For exterior areas, stone surfaces are frequently used in cities to identify a particular space and brick laid as a floor is also considered a very urban finish. Both materials can also be used to frame floor surfaces such as pavements and pedestrian zones.

In interior spaces a much thinner stone finish can be used. Traditionally flagstones (flat stones that are laid for paving surfaces) would have been used to produce a simple floor surface. Today, various types of stone are used to provide an interior floor finish, in particular limestone and marble.

Roofs

Stone can be used as a roof finish. For temperate climates a roof material that can retain heat and is impervious to water is essential. Slate is traditionally used in the UK for this purpose and is also manufactured and used in countries such as China, Mexico and Spain.

Terracotta tiles are used in many Mediterranean countries, where the traditions of both brick and pot making have been adapted and applied to roofing. Terracotta tiles can be glazed or left in their raw state.

Finishes

Stone can be left in its raw state or it can be polished to varying degrees depending on the application. Saw-cut stone has a rough finish and is most appropriate for exterior features in garden and landscape design. A honed finish is extremely smooth but not reflective, making it suitable for interior wall and floor applications. A polished finish enhances the colour of the stone and creates a smooth and reflective surface that is suitable for interior and exterior use.

The colour of brick is affected by its raw material content, for example, yellow bricks have more lime content and redder ones a higher iron content. This can provide various aesthetic options for the architect. The pattern that bricks are laid in is referred to as a 'bond' and there are many variations of these, each of which is based on context, tradition and location. The length of an exposed brick is referred to as the 'stretcher' and the shortest side of an exposed brick is a 'header'. The simplest bond, the running bond, is just continuous rows of stretcher bricks. The pattern of the bricks does not just serve a decorative function, the overlap of the bricks is essential to maintain stability in the wall.

Project: Solstice Arts Centre
Location: County Meath, Ireland
Architect: Grafton Architects
Date: 2006

The Solstice Arts Centre in Navan,
County Meath, incorporates a
theatre space, exhibition areas and
a café. Located on a sloping site,
the main building is constructed from
reinforced concrete and clad in
ashlar stone blocks. The building has
a transparent, glazed façade at
ground level, which opens onto
a public square.

Cultural and material context › **Application** › Grand master

Antonio Gaudí

Catalan architect Antonio Gaudí (1852–1926) was inspired by natural and Gothic forms, his sculptural building designs were both organic and dynamic in their expression and he was famously experimental with structural and physical forms.

Both Gaudí's buildings and concepts challenged traditional Spanish architecture. His portfolio of work includes housing blocks in Barcelona with façades that interpret structure and walls that are sculpted architectural forms. Throughout his life, Gaudí studied nature's own angles and curves and incorporated them into his designs. The hyperboloids and paraboloids he borrowed from nature were easily reinforced by steel rods and allowed his designs to resemble elements from the environment.

At Parc Güell located to the north of Barcelona, Gaudí's shapes and forms in the landscape present playful lines and surface. His work is distinct. He uses traditional local craft and building skills (such as the mosaic work in Parc Güell), but reinterprets them, mixing references to nature and abstract ideas of animal and plant forms.

La Sagrada Familia's distinctive towers

La Sagrada Familia

In his later years, Gaudí devoted his architectural energies to the designs for the Templo Expiatorio de la Sagrada Familia (La Sagrada Familia), a Roman Catholic church in the heart of Barcelona, Spain. A hugely ambitious project from the outset (and groundbreaking in terms of structural ambition), construction began in 1882 and is still to be completed today. One of its remarkable factors is that the designs were considered 'modern' in Gaudí's time, yet they somehow remain 'new' in the context of today's architecture, displaying abstract expression and challenges in structure.

The scheme is intended to have 18 towers, 12 to represent each of the Apostles (so far eight have been constructed, each with a statue of the Apostle beneath it), four more to represent the Evangelists and a tower each for the Virgin Mary and Jesus Christ. La Sagrada Familia's towers are undoubtedly the most impressive feature on the Barcelona skyline and they can also be experienced from within. The towers have staircases that wind up inside them and bridges that link from one to another, allowing incredible views over the city and beyond. The towers get thinner as one progresses, almost appearing to defy gravity. The pinnacles at the top of the towers are finished with forms inspired by plants and flowers, which are decorated in brightly coloured mosaic work.

The building design has three façades: the Nativity façade to the East, the Glory façade to the South (yet to be completed) and the Passion façade to the West. The exterior is covered with carefully designed narrative carvings, describing scenes associated with Christianity, from the nativity to the passion.

The internal plan of the building consists of five aisles with a central nave. The central vault reaches 60 metres and the apse is capped by a hyperboloid structure that reaches 75 metres. Gaudí's intention was for it to be possible for the visitor to see the vaults of the nave, crossing and apse from the main entrance, and for the vault to appear to increase in height as he or she approached the centre of the space.

An interior view of the towers

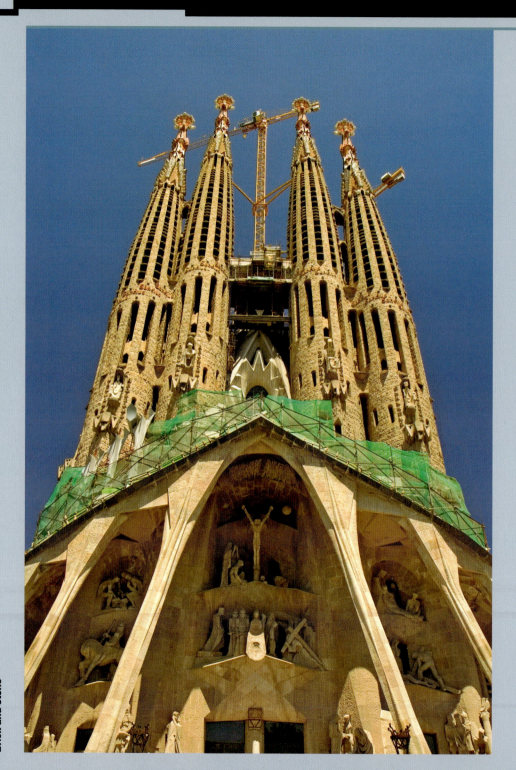

Exterior view of the entrance
and towers

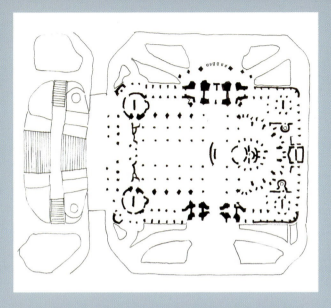

The complex ground floor plan

The cathedral's interior columns have a unique design. As
well as serving their load-bearing purpose and supporting the
towers above, they change shape from their base, which is
octagonal, slowly becoming a 16-sided shape and finishing
in a circle form.

La Sagrada Familia has been likened to a piece of three-
dimensional art or sculpture. It can be admired from a
distance as an impressive piece of engineering and form
making and it can be further explored from within. The
building was designed to challenge ideas of structure and
celebrate the most incredible craftsmanship; to carve and
transform stone from a solid, static material to a dynamic
expressive surface. This building exemplifies the potential
that stone offers the architect and the real possibility its
use presents to create symbolic, iconic and memorable
structures.

Jonathan Woolf studied architecture in Rome and in London where, for Munkenbeck & Marshall, he was project architect for the house of art collector Charles Saatchi. He established his own practice in 1990 and has taught at schools throughout the UK and Europe since 1995, including the University of Bath, the Architectural Association, London, and at Robert Gordon University in Scotland.

Woolf Architects have completed over 24 projects to date including residential houses, artist and photographer's studios, office spaces, apartments and hotels.

The design brief

The clients for Brick Leaf House, two brothers, wanted a design that incorporated a modern white building in the style of Luis Barragan, a South American architect whose work is characterised by juxtaposing light rendered walls with brightly coloured wall planes. The project planners suggested something contemporary in concrete, but Woolf Architects argued the case for using brick. This offered a possibility to work with a material that would age with the natural elements of the site and would only require limited maintenance.

Brick and stone

An exterior view of Brick Leaf House

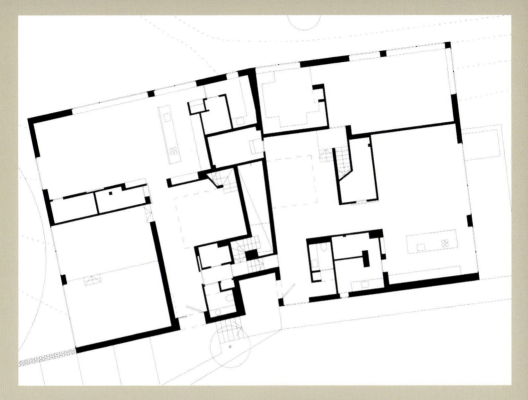

Grand master: Antonio Gaudi › Brick Leaf House › 30 Finsbury Square

'I wanted to create an urban feel, the type you get where a brick building abuts hard up against a stone road, very much like the hill towns of Italy and Spain.'
Jonathan Woolf

The design solution

Brick Leaf House (1999–2003) sits on the edge of Hampstead Heath in London. The building is located over a steeply sloping site and its only real immediate context is its garden setting. Brick Leaf House is also referred to as 'double house' because it is actually two dwellings, and was commissioned by two brothers and their respective families for use as residential accommodation.

The house's tectonic expression is very straightforward, comprising a steel frame (to allow flexibility in the internal layout) clad in an laconic brick skin. As well as being relatively low-maintenance, a key advantage of using brick for this build was that it is part of the palette of the area.

Plan showing how the two separate house spaces are divided

Views showing the relationship between the house and the surrounding gardens (above and facing page, left)**, and the external approach to the house** (facing page right)

The 'ordinariness' of this language is further reinforced by the use of off-the-shelf steel windows, the frames of which are finished in white. This building demonstrates an informal minimalism, which responds well to its context, amongst mature trees on the edge of London's Hampstead Heath.

The houses of Spanish and Italian hill towns in this scheme heavily influenced Woolf Architects in their designs for this project. Brick Leaf House is situated on a natural slope and the architects were keen to work with and exploit this element of the site. The house was originally conceived as a Palladian villa. Situated on the edge of the city, the double dwelling had sufficient surrounding area to warrant designing a grand house in this tradition. There was an intention to create an urban house in a suburban context.

At first sight, Brick Leaf House appears as one home, but there are clues (such as the two entrances and the building's outline) that it has two dwellings within it. There are clearly shared areas to this house, but each dwelling is connected only at basement level by a communal swimming pool, and there are two quite separate living spaces where the families can conduct their own private lives.

The specification for the brick used in this build is a departure from the red brick of many traditional British suburban homes. For Brick Leaf House a hand-made, mauvish brick with a bucket-handle and jointed mortar in a matching colour was specified.

Working with the building's natural context (particularly in wet weather), the brick's rich textural effect complements the wet bark of the 50-year-old copper beech trees that are planted in the surrounding garden, serving as an important visual marker for the site.

Brick Leaf House challenges the standard notion of scale in a suburban home because it is two houses that read as one within the context of a 'special' landscape. The brick is used simply, but it reads as a subtle, textured material that works with the light, shadow and the surrounding trees.

Grand master: Antonio Gaudí › Brick Leaf House › 30 Finsbury Square

Founded in 1983, Eric Parry Architects is an established and award-winning practice with a growing portfolio of work and clients. The practice has a reputation for challenging convention and for working carefully and subtly with materials. An understanding of the architectural idea manifested in the careful specification, consideration and detailing of materials lies within their work.

The design brief

Eric Parry Architects (EPA) were commissioned by investment company Scottish Widows in 1999 to develop and achieve planning approval for a new office development in Finsbury Square, London. The project is situated in a conservation area and required the demolition of a locally listed 1920s structure. The project team therefore had to carefully consider conservation issues within their design scheme and consult heavily with the local authority and local forum groups.

Brick and stone

The main elevation

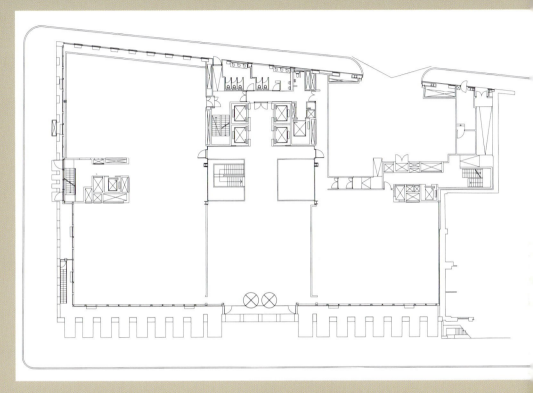

The building's ground floor plan

The design solution

This project presented something of a challenge to the EPA team. Most corporate clients want their office building to be distinct and connect directly with their commercial identity, which can be a difficult brief for any building. In addition to this requirement, the site, located as it is within a conservation area, had strict planning issues and limitations concerning the height of the building. EPA's solution had to work within a limit of six storeys (with an additional two attic storeys) and it needed to respond to the material used for surrounding buildings in the square: Portland stone.

EPA's design evolved from a study of the existing urban setting and building fabrics used. The block successfully responds to the planning and conservation limitations, but the building's elevation design reinvents the idea of the use of stone in a building façade. In this build, the Portland stone takes the form of innovative load-bearing limestone piers, which support the internal steel beams.

The façade reinterprets the idea of stacking stone, with openings staggered across each elevation (each window within the elevations varies in its location and proportion from the one above), and in doing so it challenges the convention of how stone is used in building and construction.

Behind the stone, the elevations are constructed from glass (this building is essentially a glass office block contained within a stone 'cloak'). The deep stone façade acts as a brise soleil to provide shading and reduce the amount of sunlight entering the building, which is in keeping with energy conservation requirements. As sunlight passes over the façade, the depth of the stone animates the surface, transforming it from a two-dimensional surface to a three-dimensional one.

Stone is not often used structurally in contemporary builds; its expense means that it is usually used as a cladding material instead. So in addition to this unusual, functional and perhaps luxurious use of stone for a structural application, this façade (because it bears the weight of the building's floors) also allows the interior space to be kept completely free of structure, providing flexibility for the internal planning.

This project exemplifies the large-scale use of high-quality materials and this combination creates a distinct identity for the building. EPA have successfully used materials intelligently and inventively, and in doing so have challenged the conventional idea of an office block façade in an urban, working environment. The building has won a RIBA award, an AIA/UK Design Excellence Award, a commendation from the British Council for Offices and was shortlisted for the Stirling Prize in 2003.

A view of the building wrapping around the corner of the square (facing page)**, and a detail of the stone elevation** (above)

Brick Leaf House › 30 Finsbury Square

Concrete has been used in building and construction since Roman times (the dome of the Pantheon, which dates from AD 125, was made from a form of concrete). It is a composition that can be easily mixed from sand, cement and stone, and has the potential to be both solid and fluid (and so take any shape). It is a flexible, malleable material that can be mixed to whatever consistency is required.

Concrete was once considered an industrial, rough and brutal material that was typically used to create structure rather than a finished surface and as such was commonly associated with industrial architecture. However, changing methods of construction have revealed concrete as an important material in its own right. As construction techniques have become more refined, exposed concrete surfaces have become increasingly popular in wider architectural applications and with steel reinforcement, concrete can be incredibly strong, which is why its use is favoured for superstructures such as bridges or skyscrapers.

Concrete can be pre-cast (poured in a factory), producing prefabricated elements that can be quickly assembled on site for swift and simple construction. Alternatively, it can be cast in situ (on site), to create a form or shape that responds to a mould. This flexibility allows many dynamic forms and shapes to be achieved. The container (or 'formwork') holds the concrete as it sets and in doing so leaves an impression on the surface of the material.

As technology develops, concrete becomes ever more versatile, offering architects the possibility to create ever more dynamic forms and shapes. This releases the potential for organic form in architecture and reveals concrete's ability to be subtle as well as strong. It is a truly flexible material of the 21st century.

Project: The Jewish Museum
Location: Berlin, Germany
Architect: Daniel Libeskind
Dates: 1998–2001

During the design process for Berlin's Jewish Museum, Daniel Libeskind plotted the addresses of prominent Jewish and German citizens on a map of pre-war Berlin and joined the points to form an 'irrational and invisible matrix' on which he based the language of form, the geometry and shape of the building. The museum also houses the Holocaust Tower. The bare concrete tower is 24 metres high and neither heated nor insulated. It is lit by a single narrow slit high above the ground.

AD 125
Pantheon

Rome's Pantheon is one of the earliest and most celebrated examples of a concrete building. Its crowning dome is constructed from stepped rings of concrete that sit on masonry walls. The dome's interior features an oculus from which a series of coffers (sunken panels in the ceiling) radiate.

1903
Ingalls Building
Elzner & Anderson

Situated in Cincinnati, USA, the Ingalls Building was the world's first concrete skyscraper. The building was constructed without the use of steel reinforcement and incorporated eight-inch concrete walls, and floors, beams, columns, stairs and a roof all made from concrete.

1905
Garage at 51 Rue de Ponthieu
Auguste Perret

Designed by Auguste Perret, this reinforced concrete structure spanned a large space and provided a light, open and airy interior. The concrete structure provided sufficient support for the elevation to have large openings, which allowed light to penetrate into the interior of the building.

1945
Le Havre Cathedral
Auguste Perret

The cathedral in Le Havre, northern France, formed a central part of the city's post-war redesign. The city plan was developed by Auguste Perret, and he used reinforced concrete to create remarkable structures in Le Havre including roadside colonnades and civic buildings as well as the city's cathedral.

1965
Chandigarh Urban Planning
Le Corbusier

Le Corbusier determined the urban form for this new settlement in India and was responsible for designing the key 'Special Areas' of the city, each of which contains several individual buildings. The Chandigarh project comprised a city centre, parks, a cultural complex, art gallery and college of art.

1965
The Salk Institute
Louis Kahn

The buildings in this educational complex in California are constructed from reinforced concrete, wood, marble and water. The concrete is left exposed to create the aesthetic of the buildings and the wood is used to produce a contrast with the hardness of the structure.

Concrete

1915
Lingotto Building
Giacomo Matté-Trucco

Located in Turin, Italy, the Lingotto Building is probably most famous for housing the Fiat Factory between 1923 and 1982. Built entirely from concrete, it has always been a strong poster image for early Modernism because its forms are determined by functional requirements.

1916
Orly Airport Hangars
Eugene Freyssinet

Freyssinet was the inventor of the 'prestressing' technique, which was devised to overcome difficulties in creating curved shapes in reinforced concrete. Freyssinet's hangars at Orly Airport in Paris needed to house large structures and concrete had the flexibility to provide a high, wide-spanning structure using a barrel vault construction.

1934
Penguin Pool, London Zoo
Berthold Lubetkin

Having studied the behaviour of the penguins, Lubetkin designed this pool as a pair of intertwining ramps that allowed the penguins access to the pool. They are constructed from reinforced concrete and are both sculptural and functional.

1991
Niterói Contemporary Art Museum
Oscar Niemeyer

This extraordinary museum responds to the surrounding landscape with dramatic form. Located in Niterói, Rio de Janeiro, Brazil, this building has a futuristic, space-age presence. Use of concrete gives Niemeyer the freedom to explore experimental sculptural form, influenced by geometry.

1998
La Ciudad de las Artes y las Ciencias de Valencia
Santiago Calatrava

The City of Arts and Sciences building, developed by Santiago Calatrava, is a large-scale urban recreation centre for culture and science in Valencia, Spain. The centre covers an area of 350,000 square metres. Calatrava's designs specified the use of pure white concrete and fragments of shattered tiles in the traditional Catalan style.

2007
The Museum of Modern Literature
David Chipperfield Architects

Winner of the 12th RIBA Stirling Prize and located in Marbach am Neckar, Germany, this museum was designed to display and archive works of literature from the 20th century. The construction materials reflect the museum's spaces and include fair-faced concrete, sandblasted reconstituted stone and limestone aggregate.

Project: Penguin Pool, London Zoo
Location: London, UK
Architect: Berthold Lubetkin
Date: 1934

The Penguin Pool at London Zoo successfully combines the engineering and sculptural potentials of concrete in architectural design. A pair of ramps intertwines to allow penguins to travel from different levels in the enclosure to a pool at a lower level. The ramps are made from reinforced concrete and appear to be suspended. Concrete, a characteristically 'heavy' material, appears to be 'light' in Lubetkin's design, creating a clever and carefully engineered solution.

Concrete is a mixture of sand, rock and cement (cement is the binding material that holds the rock and the sand together). Historically, concrete structures existed where these materials were present because it needed to be mixed wherever the raw materials were available. The use of 'concrete' can be seen in early forms of Egyptian architecture; for example, there is evidence of a type of cement used on a wall in Thebes, which dates back to 1950 BC. However, earlier evidence of the use of cement can be found as far back as 6500 BC (where it is believed to have been used by Syrians to create floor surfaces).

Concrete

The Romans used a form of concrete to engineer many of their impressive structures, a number of which still stand today. For example, both the Coliseum (AD c.82) and the Pantheon (AD c.126) contain large amounts of concrete, and the Basilica of Constantine and foundations of the Forum buildings also were built using concrete.

Following the Roman civilisation, there was less evidence of the use of concrete in architectural forms. Concrete had been considered as an engineering material: heavy and brutal. Many buildings that have survived from this period are those considered to be culturally valuable or celebrated for their skilled use of materials (rather than for engineering innovation).

Structural possibilities

In the late-18th and early-19th century, the Industrial Revolution triggered a new interest in engineering, innovation, structure and form. The discovery and creation of new materials in this period was to create a new form of architecture. Concrete offered the architect a material that could be moulded to form new shapes and one that, when reinforced with metal, could be used structurally to challenge ideas of building form and scale.

In 1903, the Ingalls Building was constructed in Cincinnatti, Ohio, USA. Designed by architects Elzner & Anderson it was the world's first (reinforced) skyscraper and its realisation was made possible by the use of reinforced concrete in its construction. The building was designed to house various office spaces and its elevation was in a beaux-arts style. Although the building's construction embraced innovative building techniques, its appearance was conventional for the era.

The 20th century was to see a new language of **modern architecture** develop and Modernist architects were to use concrete as their material of choice. Concrete offered possibilities for a flexible type of building shape and allowed designers to move away from an architecture defined by decoration to one of dynamic spaces and fluid shapes.

The new machines of the 20th century (such as airships, airplanes and cars) needed new structures to house them and the modern factories of early 20th-century Europe commonly used concrete for this purpose. This produced an architecture characterised by an industrial aesthetic and it is only in recent years that this brutal style has been challenged as new techniques and processes of manufacture are creating a more subtle type of concrete. These innovations mean that concrete is no longer just a heavy, hard-wearing engineering and building material; it has its own beauty and character that continues to evolve as the manufacturing processes become ever more refined.

Modern architecture

'Modern architecture' is a term given to a number of building styles with similar characteristics, primarily the simplification of form and the elimination of ornament. The style was conceived early in the 20th century. Modern architecture was adopted by many influential architects and architectural educators, however very few 'modern' buildings were built in the first half of the century. It gained popularity after the Second World War and became the dominant architectural style for institutional and corporate buildings for three decades.

Concrete

Project: Aircraft Hangar
Location: Orbetello, Italy
Architect: Pier Luigi Nervi
Date: 1940

Nervi was a trained engineer who used his understanding of materials to create incredibly elegant structures. He designed aircraft hangars that incorporated large-span, open spaces to comfortably accommodate the airplanes. He is renowned for his work on the ideas associated with the development of reinforced and prefabricated concrete technologies.

Timeline: concrete › **Origins and chronology** › Cultural and material context

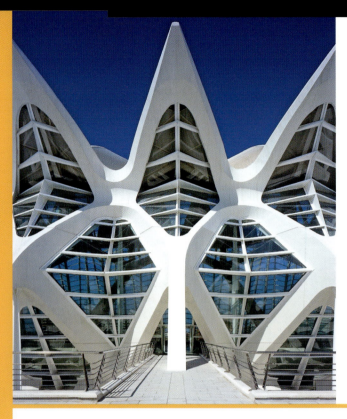

Topography

Topography is concerned with local detail in general, including not only relief but also vegetative and human-made features, and even local history and culture. This meaning is less common in America, where topographic maps with elevation contours have made 'topography' synonymous with relief. The older sense of Topography as the study of place still has currency in Europe.

Unlike other construction materials, which may strongly connect with the place of their origin, concrete is made from ingredients that can now be mixed anywhere. This not only makes it flexible in terms of manufacture, but also does not restrict the material to a particular location. This affords concrete a sense of anonymity, which means it is much less limited by traditional ideas and concepts than other materials: it can be anything, anywhere. Notwithstanding this, the use of concrete in architecture is (usually) still informed by local ideas of construction, form, function and other aspects of context.

Concrete and the era of Modernism

The prominent Modernists of the early 20th century, notably Le Corbusier and Auguste Perret, exploited the flexibility of concrete to create new forms and shapes. They designed cities for the future that contained strong, bold and tall structures all made from concrete.

Project: Chapel Notre Dame du Haut (right)
Location: Ronchamp, France
Architect: Le Corbusier
Date: 1954

Le Corbusier's Chapel Notre Dame du Haut at Ronchamp uses concrete to create a dramatic and sculptural form on both the exterior and interior spaces. The building is punctured with holes filled with coloured glass and these bring light into the chapel illuminating the interior space. The building appears as a sculptural element in the natural landscape.

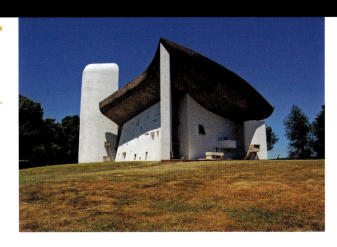

Title: Ciudad de las Artes y las Ciencias (facing page)
Location: Valencia, Spain
Architects: Santiago Calatrava
Date: 2001

The Ciudad de las Artes y las Ciencias is an urban cultural centre. It reacts to the local environment and uses white concrete to contrast with the blue Spanish skies. The concrete is used with local tile to connect the finish with traditional industries.

Continuing this tradition, Brazilian architect Oscar Niemeyer uses concrete in his designs to respond to organic forms in the landscape. Niemeyer extends the landscape and **topography** with his architectural ideas, producing dramatic shapes on rolling planes or landscapes that are made from carpets of concrete.

In South America, Luis Barragan introduced colour to his architecture to connect his building designs and materials with the traditional colours found in the landscape and culture of the region. Barragan's architecture has been described as similar to an abstract painting with wall surfaces coloured to contrast against one another and sharp coloured walls framing views across landscapes. His architecture is about the surface experience, walls that are rendered in cement and then painted, to create abstract planes.

Contemporary 21st century architecture uses concrete to create ever taller, more dramatic statements. Daniel Libeskind, for example, specified the use of concrete in his designs for Berlin's Jewish Museum to dramatise and accentuate the Jewish experience in wartime Germany, producing both a provocative and commemorative result (see page 40).

Concrete is the substance of our new buildings, our greatest edifices and our skyscrapers, and it will challenge the future of architectural forms. Yet even so, the adaptation of concrete to respond to local cultural and climatic issues is essential for its survival.

Origins and chronology › **Cultural and material context** › Application

Concrete has evolved dramatically over the last few years, using technology to create a material that is increasingly flexible in its application. Varying the manufacturing process and using new additives allows concrete to have versatile properties and offers the architect new possibilities.

There are several key characteristics to consider when using concrete in building design. It has excellent thermal mass, which means it can retain heat efficiently, and as it is a high-density material it can also absorb heat during summer (helping to cool a building), and release it again at night when the temperature drops. Another advantage is that it can be made in situ using locally sourced materials and so does not have to be transported to site (though it can also be pre-cast). Finally it is non-combustible and so can be used as a fire barrier between different layers or areas of a building.

Concrete and construction

Pre-cast/cast in situ: concrete is often available on site as 'pre-cast' pieces. These pieces are prefabricated components that can then be fitted in accordance with the architectural plans. Concrete that is cast in situ is mixed and poured into prepared formwork (or mould) on site.

Hybrid concrete construction: this is a construction method that uses both pre-cast elements and in situ formwork, allowing the project greater flexibility on site. In this method, concrete can also be sprayed onto a subframe to create a variety of spaces and surfaces.

Foundations: most buildings will have foundations that are made of concrete to provide a stable base for either a building's frame or walls. These may be simple poured strips or more complex engineered solutions using piles.

Frame: concrete is very good in compression, which means it can be used effectively to create a stable structure. Building frames can be made from pre-cast concrete and assembled on site, or poured into formwork in situ. Steel reinforcements will make the frame stronger and capable of supporting greater loads. Using concrete for the frame allows walls to be constructed from non-load-bearing materials such as glass.

Project: The Collection at Lincoln
Location: Lincoln, UK
Architect: Panter Hudspith
Architects
Date: 2005

This gallery was designed with the concrete as the defining interior surface. Panter Hudspith Architects adopted an experimental approach here by treating concrete with graphic impressions. Carefully placing leaves on to the wall surface as the concrete was setting allowed a natural and organic impression to be left on an industrial surface.

Wall: concrete walls can be constructed using formwork to create dynamic shapes, and concrete can also be used as cladding to cover existing wall surfaces. Reinforced, pre-cast concrete panels are available in many different colours and finishes (such as acid-etched, smooth, sand-blasted or polished), and various materials can be incorporated into the panels (such as marble or glass), which offers the architect a wealth of aesthetic and tactile possibilities.

Floor: many floors are made by casting a complete concrete slab at ground level, or even below ground level, which stabilises the building and provides a flat, clear surface. Intermediate floors can also be cast on site by pouring concrete into formwork. Pre-cast concrete flooring systems using concrete planks can also be used to create an immediate floor surface.

Roof: flat roofs in particular can be made and finished using concrete. A pitched roof can be made from pre-cast beams and covered with a waterproof surface or concrete slabs. Additionally dynamic shapes and forms can be achieved by casting concrete shapes for roof pieces on site.

Surface: using concrete as a surface material provides a number of opportunities for the architect. The material that is used to cast concrete can leave an impression on it. For example, timber formwork can be used to lend concrete a soft grain texture.

Project: Pavilion
Location: London, UK
Architects: Alan Dempsey and
Alvin Huang
Date: 2008

This structure was designed in
response to an Architectural
Association competition. The pavilion
utilises 13mm-thick fibre-reinforced
concrete panels and was conceived
as a prototype for testing the
structural potential of a material that
is more usually used for cladding.
The pavilion is a temporary structure
and was initially located outside
the Architectural Association's
headquarters in Bedford Square,
London.

Innovations in concrete

Grancrete: is a tough new ceramic material that is almost
twice as strong as concrete. The ceramic material is sprayed
onto a basic styrofoam frame and dries to form a lightweight
hard surface. Grancrete is fire-resistant and can withstand
both tropical and sub-freezing temperatures, making it ideal
for a range of varying climate conditions.

Hycrete: one of the crucial challenges when building with
concrete is to prevent water penetration (because concrete
is intrinsically porous and so will absorb water). Hycrete
(or waterproof) concrete is not only useful when building
below ground, but also in wet climates as it removes the
need for a membrane, allowing quicker and easier
construction methods.

Translucent concrete: Litracon is a form of light-emitting
concrete. It is produced by adding glass fibres to the
concrete mix to provide a translucent material that can be
used to construct walls or floors.

Title: Concrete floor finish
Location: Liquorish bar,
London, UK
Architect: Nissen Adams
Date: 2006

The floor aesthetic in this building resembles timber planks. However, the material used is actually concrete that has been cast to create such a finish.

Graphic concrete: it is possible to apply patterns to different concrete pieces. In addition to being patterned, the concrete surface can also have a smooth or a completely exposed fine-aggregate finish. To achieve this, a surface retarder is applied to a special membrane, which is spread over a formwork mould. The designed pattern is created by the contrast between the smooth finish and the exposed fine-aggregate finish.

The cement can also be pigmented, which provides colour for the smooth surface. The aggregates can be a variety of different colours, which are then highlighted in the exposed areas. This creates a new way to adapt the surface of the concrete panel to respond to different contexts and site conditions.

Ductile concrete: in 2005, a new type of fibre-reinforced ductile concrete was used for the first time in Michigan, USA. It looks like standard concrete, but is 500 times more resistant to cracking and 40 percent lighter in weight. Ductile concrete is made using the same ingredients in regular concrete, but without the coarse aggregate. It is engineered and reinforced with microscale fibres, which act as ligaments to bond the concrete more tightly (making it flexible).

Cultural and material context › **Application** › Grand master: Tadao Ando

Tadao Ando

Born in Osaka, Japan in 1941, Tadao Ando and his designs have been heavily influenced by 20th-century Modernism. Ando creates spaces that pay particular attention to the way in which light is controlled within them and the way in which they work in harmony with nature. This is commonly achieved via framing views and connecting the inside space of his buildings with their urban or rural exterior landscape. His designs successfully combine Japanese cultural sensitivity with an understanding of European modernism.

The process of making concrete is also something that Ando celebrates in his buildings. He uses modular shuttering (the timber frame that supports the concrete while it sets) that is based on the tatami mat (a traditional Japanese sleeping mat). The tatami mat is determined by a man's height, so this in turn lends a human scale to the architecture. Another characteristic feature of Ando's designs is that the fixings which secure the shuttering are often left exposed in the concrete wall, providing a visible reference to the construction process in the finished architecture.

Ando is an architect who understands how and when to use concrete. It can often be thought of as a dense and oppressive material. However, through careful use of openings that allow natural light to flood in his designs, Ando creates a sense of contrast between the heaviness of the material and the energy and brightness of sunlight. His architecture celebrates the use of concrete as a crafted material cast in situ. The process of casting and the finish of the surface create buildings that have a spiritual sense of place defined by substance and lightness.

Concrete

The Church of the Light's west-facing elevation

Significant projects

The Church of the Light

Tadao Ando's Church of the Light in Osaka, Japan (1988) is an example of a cultural building that embraces ideas of geometry and spirituality. Many of Ando's previous projects were simple houses constructed to make use of courtyards to bring light into the interior spaces, but geometry, minimal, modern design and the use of concrete with a high level of craftsmanship are values evident throughout his canon of work and exemplified in The Church of the Light.

The church is aptly named as the chapel is illuminated by light. The building is comprised of two rectangular volumes, that are both cut at a 15-degree angle by freestanding concrete walls. Worshippers and visitors indirectly enter the church by slipping between the two volumes. One volume contains the Sunday school and the other contains the worship hall. A cruciform cut in the concrete wall of the worship hall extends vertically from floor to ceiling and horizontally from wall to wall, aligning perfectly with the joints in the concrete. It is a simple device, but an effective definition of the space, and at night the cross creates an illuminated symbol on the outside of the church as light from within pours outside.

Both the worship hall and the Sunday school use wood to soften the interior spaces, but The Church of the Light is all about contrast. The Sunday school opens up to a double-height space with a mezzanine level and its interior utilises a lighter-coloured, smooth-finish wood. The combination of concrete and wood creates a modern, spiritual atmosphere that focuses on light within to encourage a contemplative inward experience.

The Church of the Light is superbly crafted. The smooth finish of its concrete surfaces reflect light into the interior spaces and the building reveals its construction processes via traces of the joints and bolts that held the shuttering in place, leaving tactile impressions on the smooth, grey walls.

Concrete

An interior view of the worship hall

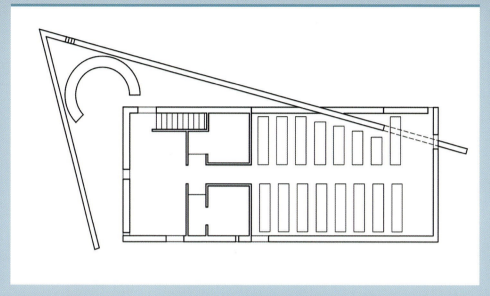

Plan showing the relationship between the worship hall's symmetrical interior and angular exterior

Ando's concrete can appear to sculpt space. To successfully achieve this it needs to be carefully moulded and controlled at each stage of its manufacture. To emulate this finish, the architect needs to understand precisely how concrete is made. Ando's is an architecture of contrasts. His interior spaces are carefully sculpted and his structural forms display powerfully defined, geometrically influenced shapes that contrast with the natural world and their surrounding landscape.

Light enters the church via apertures in the wall planes

Zaha Hadid has a reputation for challenging architectural form. Her buildings are organic, dynamic and sculptural and many of her designs spatially reinvent interior experience and exterior form. To achieve such forms, the materials Hadid uses need to be fluid, flexible, strong and beautiful, and concrete provides an extremely effective solution to these design requirements. With structural support and careful engineering, Hadid's architecture can live up to the expectations of her incredible concepts, drawings and models.

The design brief

One of Hadid's more recent projects, the BMW Central Building in Leipzig, Germany, was completed in 2005. Hadid's brief was to reinterpret the open office space and to connect this in some way with the functional demands of BMW's manufacturing and assembly environment (located on the same site) where the organisation's cars are produced. The project comprises a central building with associated fabrication volumes. The Central Building is intended to be BMW's main control and administrative centre, and the body shop, paint shop, and assembly units converge into it.

Concrete

The Central Building's elegant concrete exterior

'Architecture is really about well-being. I think that people want to feel good in a space...
On the one hand it's about shelter, but it's also about pleasure.'
Zaha Hadid

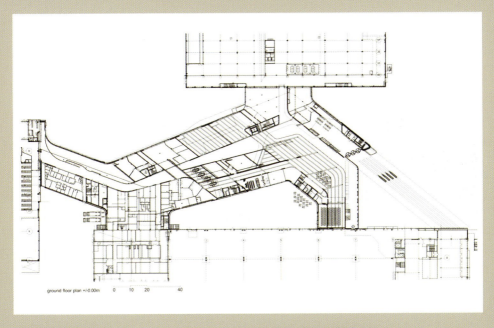

ground floor plan +/-0.00m   0   10   20   40

**The ground-floor plan
showing both the manufacturing
and administration areas of
the building**

The design solution

Hadid's solution works to juxtapose the
very different functions of the office and
manufacturing divisions; those activities
that are perhaps unseen in other plants
are celebrated in this building's design.
This building facilitates and encourages
the integration of different functions and
operatives within the building.

The large glazed lobby allows views right into
the building (revealing the manufacturing
processes), and courtyards puncture through
the building's deep plan to allow daylight into
the main spaces. The ground and first floor
are interconnected to create one continuous
landscape; these planes appear much like
a terrace and move through the building.

**The building's interior spaces
are dramatic, fluid and sculptural**
(above and facing page)

The first plane runs from the lobby and extends up to the first floor (in the middle of the building), the other begins at the cafeteria and moves into the main entrance area. These planes define the spaces and voids above, beneath and between them. Cars move through these voids as they travel along their assembly line, again connecting the main function of the building back to the entrance area and lending a transparent quality to the main building.

This building has an ambition to bring together disparate functions and activities using dynamic sculptural form. It is an environment that is unreservedly industrial and this is in harmony with the use of concrete for the build. An additional advantage is that concrete allows giant planes and landscapes to be moulded and produce an organic, sculpted shape.

Concrete

To achieve this form, the building design was originally drawn in CAD and drawing information was then used to determine the complex shapes and forms that had to be created in reinforced concrete. The beauty of the building is that its form is a piece of carefully considered engineering. Such a design requires a hierarchy of structural consideration. At the first level is the 'superstructure': the main supporting structure of the architecture. The secondary elements follow and finally the finished elements complete the hierarchy.

The Central Building's superstructure is made of precast and prestressed concrete slabs that are supported on precast concrete beams and columns. The ground floor consists of a mesh fabric, reinforced concrete slab that is built directly off the ground. The first-floor slab is supported on precast concrete columns that are based on a 10x10 metre grid. This slab consists of 450mm prestressed concrete double-T units spanning between main floor beams. The area of first-floor slab, which cuts across at an angle in front of the main entrance, has a clear span in excess of 45 metres.

The Central's Building's dramatic spaces require the structure to span large distances, and this requires specialist bridge-building technology and engineering. Five thin columns form an A-frame support at one end of the span whilst a simple vertical wall incorporated into the adjacent car plant building provides support at the other end. In situ reinforced concrete walls surround the stair and lift cores and these serve as main bracing elements to assist lateral stability and prevent the structure from folding or deforming. In addition to providing lateral stability to the structure, these walls also provide vertical support to the first-floor and roof-slab elements.

The Central Building is a piece of carefully considered and beautifully detailed architecture. It uses structural bridge-building concepts and technology to achieve large spans that create exciting voids throughout the building. The design exploits the possibilities of concrete, which it enhances by the knowledge that there is a structural necessity to every part of the building and nothing is superfluous.

'Architecture can't change the way things work. But it can create a place for rest, a place for silence. And it can do it even now that stones aren't as solid as they used to be in days when faith was something more eternal, like the faiths of Saqqara and Giza.'
Axel Schultes

Axel Schultes believes in an architecture that could last for ever. Rather than creating temporary solutions, Schultes champions architecture of permanence and substance. He wants architecture to be emotional and affect the soul, believing it has to strike a balance between freedom and necessity. Many of his buildings are clearly influenced by ancient architectural forms, buildings that have a solidity, a sense of purpose and a clear function. Schultes Frank Architects created the urban master plan for the Spreebogen (the government and parliament quarter) in Berlin as well as the city's Chancellery building.

The design brief

Designed by Axel Schultes and Charlotte Frank, and completed in 1998, Baumschulenweg Crematorium is situated in south-east Berlin, Germany. Schultes and Frank's scheme was a competition-winning entry that successfully responded to an existing building and surrounding gardens. To realise their design was a task that required tenderness, but not sentimentality.

Concrete

Exterior view from the south-west of the crematorium

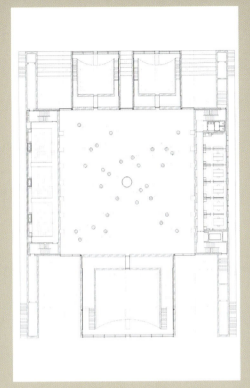

The crematorium's floor plan

The design solution

This crematorium is a place for both the living and the dead. Cremation or traditional funeral ceremonies can take place in the building and it provides a serene, controlled environment for the ritual of commemorating the death of a loved one. The intention with this building was to suggest a more secular or neutral place to allow for the reflection and contemplation of those who have passed away.

The crematorium is located within a formal woodland area. The new building is reached via a main axis, which immediately connects it with its surrounding landscape, presenting a symmetrical façade on approach. On entering, the sky and woodland can be seen beyond the building. The design of the internal hall suggests an abstraction of the forest as irregularly placed columns appear as a grove of trees, which are enhanced by light streaming in from above.

The intention with this building was to create a respectful and calm space; a place where the architecture could be invisible and silent. The building materials and structure were an important part of realising this. The main hall's structural support is provided by reinforced concrete columns (29 support the main roof); the roof and floor are concrete and the walls are finished in polished concrete. Glass is used to bring light into the space from above and to animate the surface of the columns and walls.

Despite its large-scale use, the concrete's finish is not refined and its imperfections suggest both a sense of memory and a human quality. The natural light entering the space highlights the texture and surface of the concrete, which brings depth to an otherwise flat surface.

Concrete

The enclosed columnar hall creates the character for the entire crematorium; it is both monumental and ceremonial, evoking a sense of spirituality through its control of light and space. The hall's 29 concrete columns appear to rise from the ground at irregular intervals and give structure to the rectangular-shaped space. Rings of daylight define the top of these columns giving the impression that the roof is floating above rather than fixed on to the supporting pillars. Cantilevered brackets at the top of each column allows the roof to 'hover' over this space much like a translucent canopy.

A round pool lies within this 'forest' of pillars, reflecting light and animating the surrounding space. This is a space that is both simple and complex and provides an experience that uses material and light to suggest a calm, contemplative area, a place in which to reflect and consider.

The cremation rooms on the basement floor are accessed via two ramps at the back of the building. Separated from the rooms where the funeral services are held, they are kept out of the mourners' view and the only visible signs of them from the outside are three stacks that are aligned along one side of the roof.

The funeral services are held in one of the building's three chapels. These are accessible from the building's main façade, via two niches that run the full height of the building.

Interior views of the columnar hall
(facing page and above)

The Central Building › Baumschulenweg Crematorium

Timber is a versatile building material. It can be used to create a building's skeleton structure or be utilised to great effect for internal and external finishes. It's possible to design and construct a building entirely of timber, from its frame and wall coverings to the roof. In addition to its versatility, timber is the ultimate sustainable material. If properly sourced it can be grown, used and replenished with little or no waste from its manufacture and production.

Timber also offers the architect more than just practical advantages; it is an aesthetically rich material that can vary depending on a tree's species and type. Additionally, it has a natural beauty that (over time) can weather, a feature which can gradually add to a design scheme.

Different finishing techniques that further cultivate the beauty of timber are also at the architect's disposal. For example, it may be sanded, smoothed, waxed, varnished, stained or painted. A timber finish is ultimately flexible and can be adapted to suit a great number of possibilities, tastes and applications.

Timber architecture has often been most associated with those countries that have plentiful natural sources of it (such as Canada or Scandinavian countries), but in recent years timber-framed designs have become more commonplace in a range of countries. The eco-friendly and sustainable houses that make good use of timber in their design are the smart houses of the future.

Project: Peninsula House
Location: Victoria, Australia
Architect: Sean Godsell
Dates: 2002

Sean Godsell's Peninsula House is dug into the side of a sand dune on a beach south of Melbourne. It is an apparently simple exercise in Jarrah timber and light, sun and sea. But it is made with subtlety and detailed care.

Concrete › **Timber** › Glass and steel

c.5000 BC
Neolithic house

The farmers of Central and Western Europe first introduced this style of Neolithic longhouse around 5000 BC. Very few examples remain simply because timber does not preserve well. The example shown here is a reconstruction, but the connection between the style of the house and the form of a Viking ship is clearly visible; it's likely that the same craftsmen would have worked on both ships and buildings.

c.3100 BC
Stonehenge

In 2005 timber structures were discovered at Stonehenge (in Wiltshire, England), which are thought to be the remains of the builders' living quarters (used whilst the stone structures were being built). These are some of the oldest timber structures that survive.

1400–1500
Wealden Hall houses

Wealden Hall houses were constructed in Kent and Sussex, England for the yeoman class (gentleman-farmer). They combined all elements of lodgings under a single roof. This neat solution paved the way for later timber-framed blocks. Earlier examples of these houses have a recessed central section representing a double-height hall, which was lit by a large window at one end.

1804
Timber windmill

The windmill pictured is located in Leisele, Alveringem, West-Flanders, Belgium. Old windmills, made entirely from local timber, have been in use since the 12th century here. They are a part of the landscape and enabled the land to be drained.

1972
Timber-framed Huf Haus
Peter Huf

German company Huf Haus specialises in creating individually crafted homes that combine beautiful architecture with environmentally sound building practices. All aspects of the house are made in a factory then shipped to sites around the world. In 1972 Huf Haus developed its timber-framed house, which has an open plan interior.

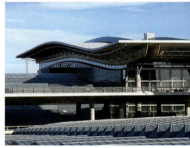

1988
Oslo Airport
Aviaplan

The main terminal building of Oslo's Gardermoen Airport was designed by the Aviaplan group (including Niels Torp, Narud Stokke Wiig and Skaarup & Jespersen), and uses timber to incredible structural and aesthetic effect. It is believed to be the world's only major airport with a wooden structure and is the largest laminated structure in the world.

1600s
Complex façades

During the 17th century timber-framed façades become very complex. This was attributed to a developing aesthetic preference for extra decoration rather than a need for any additional structural pieces. The Feathers Hotel in Ludlow, Shropshire (shown here) is a classic example of this style.

1700s
Medieval jetties

This street in York, England, demonstrates the aesthetic effect that the application of overhanging timber jetties achieved. This was an architectural feature that was extremely popular between the 14th and 17th centuries.

c.1700–1800
Farmstead log cabin

Log cabins were commonplace dwellings in many parts of North America and Canada during the 18th century. Most were similar in their design and were usually built in heavily wooded areas using felled logs that were simply stacked and interlocked. Roofs were constructed from cut and shaped timber shingles (or tiles).

2006
Welsh Assembly Building
Richard Rogers Partnership

The Senedd was designed by the Richard Rogers Partnership and uses traditional Welsh materials such as slate and Welsh oak in its construction. The design is based around the concepts of openness and transparency, and is also designed to be as environmentally sound as possible.

2006
The Alnwick Garden Visitor Centre
Hopkins Architects

The roof of this visitor centre is a timber diagrid structure that is covered with transparent PTFE pillows. The structure is made from solid larch sections that are bolted together at intersections with steel plates and fixings.

2007
Moonah Links lodges
Hayball Leonard Stent Architects

Winner of the 2007 Australian Timber Design Awards, the Moonah Links lodges are located at the Moonah Golf Resort on the Mornington Peninsula in Victoria, Australia. They use timber for decorative effect; mixing rough sawn timber with planed timber to give a natural finish.

Historically, timber buildings have not survived the ravages of time incredibly well. The properties of timber make those buildings constructed wholly from it vulnerable to rot, fire and general wear and tear. As such, timber buildings do not have the lasting history of their stone, brick or concrete counterparts. However, it is the 'temporary' nature of timber buildings that characterises their architecture, and this is further enhanced by those crafts and skills that have developed and evolved to respond to the timber tradition.

The past

The earliest timber buildings include Neolithic longhouses, which were commonly found in Europe around 5000 BC. This building type was a timber-framed construction made with locally sourced timber. Neolithic longhouses subsequently influenced the development of medieval houses in Europe and Scandinavia.

In the medieval period, timber frame structures were enhanced with infill panels made by weaving willow and lighter timbers to make wattle and daub (the lattice of wooden strips is called the 'wattle', and this is 'daubed' with a sticky material usually made of some combination of wet soil, clay, sand, animal dung and straw). All the materials were locally sourced and easily replaced and repaired. In earlier buildings of this period the use of timber was purely functional, but in later buildings both the structure and infill panels became much more decorative.

During the mid-16th century, brick became a popular architectural material of substance and permanence. Often timber-framed buildings were clad with a thin layer of brickwork to transform the appearance of the architecture.

The industrial revolution in the mid-18th century created a transport system of canals that allowed heavy materials to be transported long distances. Before this, building materials had had to be sourced locally (which promoted the use of timber as a viable architectural material). This advance led to a period of decline for timber buildings; however, during the 19th century, the Victorian architecture referred back to the medieval past and used faux timber framing (which was painted black) to suggest that the buildings were older than they really were.

Timber

The present

In much contemporary architecture the use of timber has become increasingly appropriate as the building industry responds to the sustainable sourcing and application of materials debate. Timber is becoming more adaptable in its use, more readily specified in mass building and the carpentry and joinery skills needed to construct timber-framed buildings are now being rediscovered. Crucially, timber is a crop and as such it can be grown to replace and generate future reserves; this makes timber one of the most sustainable materials in the construction industry. As such, timber has responded well to the social and economical issues associated with construction and materials.

Project: Little Moreton Hall
Location: Cheshire, UK
Architect: Unknown
Dates: 1450–1580

This Tudor manor house is a fine example of a timber-framed building. It uses oak for the main structure and the panels are wattle and daub (a timber lattice infilled with a clay and animal dung mixture). The building's oak frame is expressive and clearly visible (because it is accentuated by black paint). The timber is also decorative and uses square panels with different patterns to create a distinctive facade.

Project: Felix Nussbaum Museum
Location: Osnabrück, Germany
Architect: Daniel Libeskind
Date: 1998

The Felix Nussbaum Museum is an extension to the Cultural History Museum in Osnabrück and is dedicated to the work of the German artist. The building's exposed reinforced concrete and aluminium structure is clad with timber. The scheme consists of three main components: a tall and narrow central corridor, a long main section, and a bridge, which acts as a connection to the Cultural History Museum.

Timber

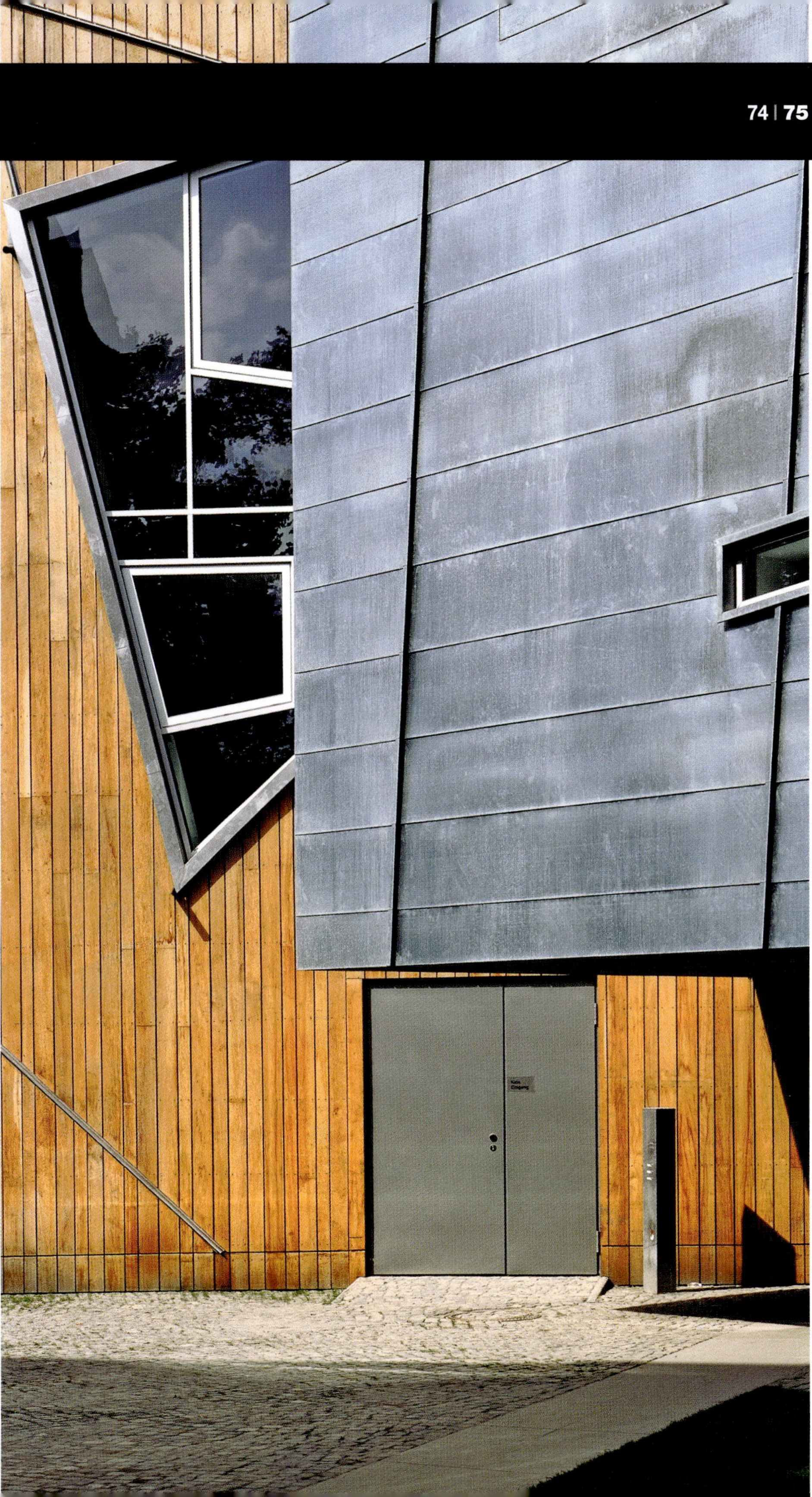

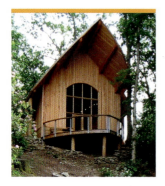

Project: David Douglas Pavilion
Location: Pitlochry, Scotland
Architect: Gaia Architects
Dates: 2003

Gaia Architects have a reputation
for their integrated and ecologically
sensitive approach. This pavilion
is made entirely from locally sourced
Scottish timber. It was designed
to commemorate the 19th-century
explorer and one of the founders
of the Scottish forestry industry,
David Douglas.

Unsurprisingly, timber buildings are most commonly associated with those countries that hold rich natural reserves of the material. The European Alps, Scotland, North America and in particular, Scandinavia have influenced and informed generations of architectural expression.

Timber is a natural building material choice in Norway where a third of the country's surface area is covered by forests. The material is readily available and there is a strong tradition and skilled craftsmanship associated with woodworking. In Finland and Sweden the simple cabin structure was the first vernacular timber building. These were traditionally built using log construction techniques and the region's extensive coniferous forests offered a plentiful supply of timber. Wooden churches were also commonly built in north-west Finland; for example, some church buildings in Turku (Finland's oldest and fifth largest city) date back to 1150.

There is a practicality to the way that timber buildings are built; with skill they can be easily constructed and are quick to repair. Timber buildings have a warmth that comes from the colour and texture of the material itself, but they can also be constructed to provide a physically warm environment.

Buildings made from timber are heavily influenced by tradition and craft, but they can also connect to contemporary cultural ideas. In architectural practice today, the concept of 'craft' is enjoying a period of renaissance and how the material references its origin is a key aspect of this.

Project: Muuratsalo Experimental House
Location: Lake Päijänne, Finland
Architect: Alvar Aalto
Dates: 1952–1954

Shown above is a smoke sauna that forms part of **Alvar Aalto**'s Muuratsalo Experimental House complex. The sauna was constructed on stones that were specifically selected from the shore by Aalto and the building's logs were obtained from trees felled on the site. A special type of timber blocking was used in the construction of the sauna. The idea is always to turn the narrower ends of the round logs in the same direction in order to achieve a firm result.

Alvar Aalto

Finnish architect Alvar Aalto (1898–1976) championed the use of timber in his designs. In 1939 he constructed the Finnish Pavilion for an exhibition in New York. This 'symphony in wood' connected aspects of the Finnish landscape with a complete reinvention of timber architecture. The pavilion demonstrated what was possible with timber and proved that it could take on a variety of shapes and forms. Organic forms and use of natural materials became signatures of Aalto's work.

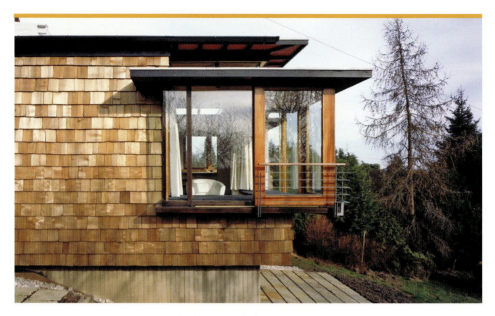

Project: MacFarlane House
Location: Glasgow, Scotland
Architect: Studio KAP
Date: 2002

Studio KAP extended this villa to
take greater advantage of its
spectacular setting. The building's
main entrance (at pavement level)
gives way to a spatial sequence that,
without changing levels, reveals a
treetop setting to the rear. The
building is covered in shingles (split
pieces of wood), which blend subtly
with the natural surroundings.

**Timber and timber products can be applied in many
different contexts; from a building's structure or frame
to boarding and cladding for walls, to construct a roof
or to produce purpose-made elements such as stairs
or window frames. Traditionally, a carpenter would have
worked with timber on site, cutting and jointing as the
designs or architect specified. Nowadays, however, the
use of timber in building demands an understanding of
how prefabricated elements that are created off site are
assembled together on site. Ease and speed of assembly
are key factors in timber-framed buildings today.**

In the construction industry, timber is graded in different
ways and these grades determine whether the wood
is used for structural purposes or for finishes. It is also
supplied in standard sizes and these are determined by
the manufacturing process. For structural timbers the
standardisation is determined by the timber's sectional size
and for sheet materials by its panel size. When designing
a building it is important that the architect is aware of these
standards so the building components will fit together
correctly and easily.

Cultural and material context › **Application** › Grand master: Edward Cullinan

Project: The Millennium Hut
Location: Glasgow, Scotland
Architect: Studio KAP
Date: 1999

Located within a new public space as part of Glasgow's 1999 'Five Spaces' initiative, the Millennium Hut was designed by Studo KAP in collaboration with artist Claire Barclay to provide a much needed community facility. The structure uses timber as a frame and cladding, with shingles and timber boarding as an external skin.

Structural frame

Structural framing forms the shape of a building. It is generally hidden behind the internal and external cladding and so is rarely seen except during construction (although it can be left exposed if the architectural idea is to celebrate the material and form of the building). Framing typically uses a number of closely spaced parallel elements to support large areas of lining or cladding. Timber framing can be used for walls, ceilings, floors, partitions and a building's roof because it (generally) has the ability to bridge small to medium spans and carry light loads.

Engineered timber can increase the structural strength of framework. For example, metal connectors and fittings or glue-laminated timber (layers of wood that are carefully glued together) can create strong structural components that need not be restricted by raw timber sizes and can be used in large-scale projects.

Timber

Roof frame

A timber roof frame will comprise several elements. These include triangular truss units, which are connected to the walls and also tied to one another for structural stability; rafters that serve as beams and are laid to support the roof; and joists that are laid at regular intervals from wall to wall and provide constant support for the ceiling or the floor. Finally, purlins are horizontal structural elements that support the rafters; these need to be carefully supported by structural walls.

Flooring and decking

Timber can be used for both the floor frame and as a floor finish. The floor finish can be achieved using pieces of solid timber or wood layered on top of a composite board. Either laminated or solid timber floor pieces can be supplied in a range of colours and lacquers.

Decking is a type of timber board flooring, and each board is structural rather than decorative. Decking is commonly used externally in gardens, marinas, bridges, pier structures and footbridges.

Panelling

Timber panels can offer structural rigidity in a timber-framed building, provide support for a floor surface or roof finish or they can be used decoratively as an interior or exterior finish. This sort of versatility requires a range of timber products that are specifically designed to suit different functions. Examples include plywood, tongue and groove, particle- or oriented-strand board or solid wood.

An important consideration with all timber panelling is to ensure that there is adequate ventilation. Any wood products used externally need to be regularly maintained as the material finish will naturally discolour and deteriorate.

Project: Cliveden Village
Location: Berkshire, UK
Architect: Onko Architects
Date: 2008

This building has timber shakes
(slices of timber used as a protective
edge) applied to its end wall. The
timber specified for the shakes was
sweet chestnut, which will weather
over time to a soft grey colour.

Timber

External cladding

Buildings can be clad with a range of different timber applications, such as solid boards or shingles, to suit a variety of functional demands. Another advantage of using timber to clad buildings is that it can be designed to suit most environments and fit most sites with a minimum of expense. To deal with varying weather conditions different coating systems can be applied to timber to protect its finish. As well as prolonging the life of the material, these systems can be used to quickly and effectively change the colour and style of the building.

Open-vented timber rainscreens have become a popular form of cladding in much contemporary architecture. These outer screens allow the rain to drain away from the building (beneath it will be an airspace and a watertight wall system) and can provide an interesting aesthetic to the architecture.

Stairs

Primarily, a staircase is a functional, structural element in a building that allows movement between levels, but it can also form a decorative feature (for example, it may be free-standing or sculptural). It may be made completely from timber or just some of its component parts, such as the treads, balusters or handrail could be made from wood. Often stairs that are made out of steel or concrete will have a wooden handrail, as there is a warmth to the materiality of this.

Edward Cullinan

Since its foundation in 1965, Edward Cullinan Architects has earned a reputation for designing carefully composed, award-winning and innovative buildings. They are committed to the idea that a successful building is one that responds thoughtfully and gracefully to their clients' needs and to its local context.

Over his long career Edward (Ted) Cullinan has drawn on modernism's social ideals, nature and natural forms to create a highly personal and inventive architecture. He studied at Cambridge University and the Architectural Association at a time when the discipline was starting to broaden its range of reference. On graduating Cullinan joined the office of Sir Denys Lasdun and then continued his studies at the University of California at Berkeley in the early 1960s.

Throughout his career, Cullinan has worked to ensure a holistic approach to building production. Sustainability and consultation have been central to his practice's building techniques long before they became widely popular and he has successfully developed a strong connection to the natural environment with his sustainable objectives. Central to all of his projects is an inventive, innovative rethinking of building material application and assembly and it is this that has characterised his work.

The timber-clad roof
of the Downland Gridshell

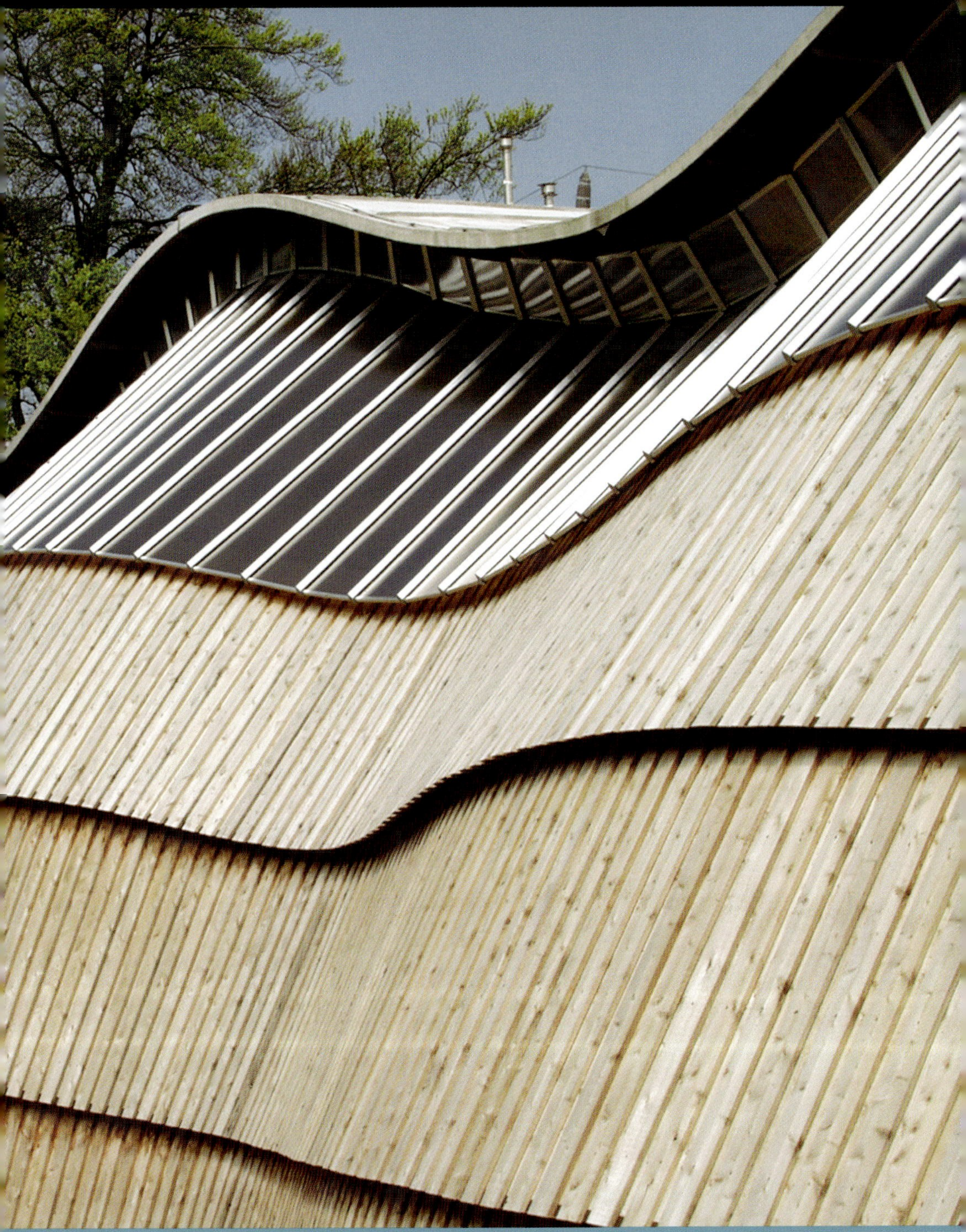

The Gridshell's exterior skin is
covered in cedar timber panels

The Downland Gridshell

Located in Singleton, West Sussex, the Weald and Downland Museum houses numerous 'real' examples of British medieval buildings ranging from a market hall and a series of individual houses to several barns that are now used for displays and exhibitions. The exhibits display particular aspects of carpentry, construction and specialist building techniques, which may inform current and future ideas of architecture and building.

Edward Cullinan Architects (ECA) were asked to add a workshop and education centre to the existing museum complex, the design for which would need to respond to the museum's collection of buildings and reinforce its aim to explain design concepts and building techniques through architectural forms. The space needed to be large enough to reassemble and display salvaged medieval timber-framed buildings and house workshops, teaching sessions and display spaces. ECA's response to this was the concept of a rural 'barn' (or gridshell) that could be built as a functional enclosure.

A gridshell is a structure that has the shape and strength of a double-curvature shell, but has a grid form instead of a solid surface. The Downland Gridshell was the first of its kind in the UK and employed a new range of construction and manufacturing techniques. It was designed and developed by engineers Buro Happold, ECA and the Green Oak Carpentry Company using CAD technology to enable advance modelling of the building's structure and form.

The Downland Gridshell is made from oak laths or strips. To prepare the oak laths for use, all defects were first removed and the resulting pieces were then finger-jointed together into standard lengths of six metres. Six of these were then joined to form 36-metre lath pieces. A diagonal grid of laths was initially formed flat on top of a supporting scaffold. The edges of the grid were then lowered gradually and the grid bent into shape until the full shell was formed and secured. The grid is actually a double layer, with two laths positioned in opposite directions, this is necessary in order to combine the required degree of flexibility with sufficient cross-section for strength. A fifth layer triangulates the grid to increase its stiffness.

Significant projects

1962–65   Cullinan House, London, England

1985   Lambeth Community Care Centre, London, England

1990   RMC International Headquarters, Surrey, England

1992   Fountains Abbey Visitor Centre, Yorkshire, England

1997   Archaeolink Visitor Centre, Aberdeenshire, Scotland

1996–99   University of East London Docklands Campus, London, England

1999   Cookson-Smith House, London, England

1996–03   Cambridge University Centre for Mathematical Sciences, Cambridge, England

2000   Greenwich Millennium School and Health Centre, London, England

2002   Downland Gridshell, Weald and Downland Museum, West Sussex, England

Application › Grand master: Edward Cullinan › The Carter/Tucker House

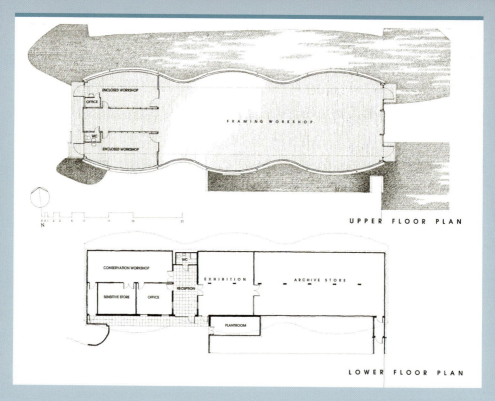

UPPER FLOOR PLAN

LOWER FLOOR PLAN

Lower and upper floor plans

The Gridshell's construction method is clearly expressed in the building. Timber pieces create the roof pattern and the bolt and plate fixings form part of the shell's interior surface. The exterior of the building is covered in cedar timber panels blending it with the surrounding woodland to such a degree that it appears to become part of it.

The Downland Gridshell is one of a very small number of gridshell structures in Britain, and both its design and method of construction are unique. Highly skilled carpentry realised its fabrication, emulating but not imitating the traditional framed buildings at the museum. This building exemplifies innovation in design via a sensitivity and understanding of the project's client, context and surrounding natural environment.

Timber

The main entrance to the Gridshell

Application › Grand master: Edward Cullinan › The Carter/Tucker House

Sean Godsell (b.1960) is one of Australia's leading architects and his work is renowned for its spare industrial forms and innovative use of materials. Trained at the University of Melbourne, Godsell travelled through Europe and Asia in the early and mid 1980s and then spent two years working in London with Sir Denys Lasdun. He subsequently returned to Melbourne to work for the Hassell Group and in 1994 opened his own practice. Godsell has built a reputation in particular for his residential architecture.

The design brief

Sean Godsell was asked to create a new residential build in the extreme landscape and climate of Australia's outback. Godsell wanted to produce a design and use construction materials that could mediate the region's hot climate and at the same time ensure that the client could take advantage (in terms of views and the relationship to outdoor space) of the landscape surrounding the house. In addition to this the client requested flexibility of the building's internal layout to allow an adaptable living space. In terms of material specification, a sensitivity to the landscape would be required to ensure that the architecture was read as part of its surroundings.

Timber

A conceptual sketch
of the Carter/Tucker house

The design solution

Embedded in a sand dune in Victoria, Australia, Godsell's Carter/Tucker House (1998–2000) takes the form of a glass box that is clad with slender cedar panels. Fulfilling the client's requirement for flexible accommodation, the house has three levels. A single space on the lower ground floor can be divided into two rooms by a sliding wall if required. Another single space on the middle level can also be divided to separate the owner's bedroom from a small sitting area. The top floor is an area for living and eating.

On all three levels the building's outer timber screen (or skin) tilts open via a system of adjustable louvres and by doing so forms an awning on the perimeter of the house. This allows the horizontal plane of the ceiling to extend beyond the building line. The screen

is made from thin strips of cedar that are positioned horizontally on a light steel frame. The screen softens the outside edge of the building, blurring it into the surrounding landscape and providing a subtle interface between the inside and outside. The entire building has been designed to weather and allow the region's climate and environment to play a positive role over time.

The changing angles of the screen's louvres constantly modify the building's appearance (depending upon the position of the viewer), and this is a conscious attempt to accentuate the buoyancy of intermittent light changes and conditions throughout the day. Light enters (or is prevented from entering) the building in an ever-changing way.

Timber

Exterior view showing how the cedar screen clads the building

As well as filtering light, the panels can be opened and shut at various points to allow an interaction between the interior and exterior of the building and provide the client with different views over the course of the day.

The Carter/Tucker House also responds to ideas that are commonly associated with the Australian vernacular. For example, the house is surrounded by a verandah, which can be partially enclosed with flywire or glass to form an indoor/outdoor space. Depending on the time of the year the verandah can then be enclosed with sliding flyscreens to become a sunroom or left open as a porch.

'I have two responsibilities as an architect: one is to be true to myself and be an artist of the utmost integrity, which is what I've tried to do. Another way of putting that is, once you're a hooker, you're a hooker for life. You can't prostitute yourself and build a building and say I didn't mean to do that one because buildings tend to stay there. The other responsibility is to be a really vigilant and analytical observer of society – by doing so we remain relevant to society.'
Sean Godsell

The interior spaces are strongly connected to views of the landscape

Grand master: Edward Cullinan › The Carter/Tucker House › The Savill Building

Formed in 1990, Glenn Howells Architects (GHA) has quickly established a strong track record in the design and delivery of its projects. The practice prides itself on being governed by four key principles: vision, responsibility, delivery and experience. Characteristic of both the practice's designs and its approach are a commitment to creativity, innovation and collaboration as well as a desire to seriously consider the integrity and impact of their architecture on the surrounding environment and immediate community. These have served GHA well as the practice now boasts a long list of satisfied clients and a range of prestigious design awards.

The design brief

The British Crown Estate commissioned GHA to design a new visitor centre that would serve as a gateway for Windsor's Great Park. The building needed to accommodate a range of visitor facilities and respond sensitively to the landscape around it. The sourcing and specification of materials was another key aspect of this build. Where possible local and sustainable resources were to be incorporated in the design scheme and traditional engineering and craft skills be used in the building's construction.

Timber

Exterior view of the Savill Building

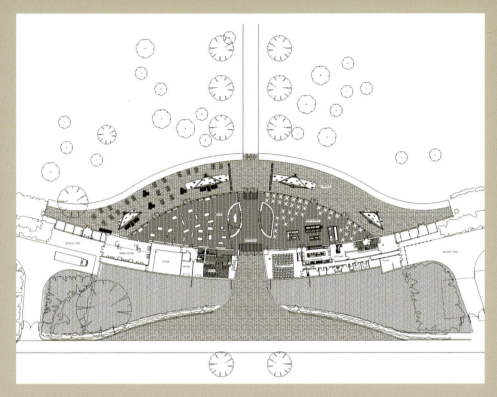

The centre's floor plan

The design solution

Opened in 2006, The Savill Building is GHA's award-winning visitor centre located in the south-eastern section of Windsor's Great Park. The centre provides an entrance to The Savill Garden and has become a unique man-made landmark within the park's natural surroundings.

The pavilion-like building takes the form of a dramatic gridshell structure and houses visitor facilities such as a ticket office, shop, self-service restaurant, seminar rooms, offices and a small garden centre all under one gently undulating roof. On entering the building the visitor's eye is drawn upwards to the roof structure, which appears to hover over the internal facilities.

'The Savill Building, designed by Glenn Howells Architects, has certainly provided us with a magnificent new iconic building that forms the entrance to the Savill Garden and gateway to the Royal landscape.'
Roger Bright, The Crown Estate

Combining contemporary engineering techniques with traditional craft skills, The Savill Building is a landmark structure and has been designed to reflect the character and quality of the surrounding gardens through its form and material application. GHA worked closely with the design team and client to create a sustainable building by making innovative use of traditional materials sourced on the estate itself.

European larch was used for the roof structure and this timber was sourced from Forest Stewardship Council (FSC) plantations in Windsor Forest on The Crown Estate. After sampling and testing, larch was specified, as it was thought to be the best available timber from a local source that would meet the strength requirements of the build.

Timber

The pavilion's undulating roof

The structural timber was rigorously graded to meet the specification requirements, but the roof design allowed the reuse of lower grade timber in less critical areas, thereby obtaining the maximum useful yield from the resource.

The Crown Estate's woodlands at Windsor also supplied English oak for the building's rainscreen and timber floor. English oak was selected for maximum durability and also for its appearance (it weathers naturally to a silvery-grey finish). Other timber structural elements specified for the roof were spruce LVL (laminated veneer lumber) from Scandinavia and birch plywood (which was treated to prevent surface spread of flame/fire).

The building's gridshell roof in plan is 90 metres long, 25 metres at its widest and 8.5 metres at its tallest. To construct it, four layers of timber were first laid out flat and then manipulated into a doubly curved shell form. The manipulation technique uses identical components (timber laths and shear blocks), which were brought together on site. The curved shell was braced in plane, for shear strength and stiffness, by the birch plywood sheathing that supports the roof insulation and outer cladding, thus making the skin of the shell multifunctional.

The Savill Building is the UK's first free-standing gridshell complex and its rippling and visually compelling roof is approximately four times the size of that of the Downland Gridshell (see pages 84–89). This is demonstrative of the advances that have been made, over a relatively short period of time, in building technologies and techniques and the way in which architectural concepts and designs for such structures can be moved forward in light of these.

The Carter/Tucker House › The Savill Building

Glass and steel represent a manufactured form of architecture; these are materials that are used frequently in contemporary architecture to produce buildings that are both functional and practical. Yet the aesthetic possibilities with glass and steel are impressive; the architecture that utilises these materials can become almost invisible, framing views of landscape or sky, or transport us to the height of a bird soaring above a city.

Before the use of steel in architecture became commonplace, the weight of the building material and the forces of gravity and compression defined a structure and its architectural possibilities. Advances in the use of steel-frame forms brought with it a new conceptual way of thinking about structures. As steel has tensile strength, it allows new structural systems (such as cantilevers) and far-reaching aesthetic possibilities (such as gravity-defying skyscrapers) to be developed.

Methods in the manufacture and engineering of glass have also evolved. Glass is no longer limited to taking the form of a transparent surface that is held by a steel frame. Nowadays, it has the potential to be structural, creating an almost invisible architecture in the process.

Historically, glass and steel were used as interdependent materials in architectural forms. However, as glass technology has evolved, the architecture that incorporates it is becoming less and less dependent on steel for its structural integrity. Glass is a material of the future and provides both practical and symbolic qualities of transparency, lightness and openness.

Project: German Bundestag dome
Location: Berlin, Germany
Architect: Foster + Partners
Date: 1999

The dome of the Reichstag was reinterpreted by Foster + Partners by incorporating a glass cupola that punches through the building's structure. The dome offers views up to the sky above and also into the debating chamber below. The use of glass symbolically opens the Reichstag up to the German people creating a transparent architecture that is intended to reflect the transparency of the democratic values that the building houses.

1851
Crystal Palace
Joseph Paxton

Using an iron frame and glass panels, Paxton's Crystal Palace was the world's first prefabricated glass building. It was constructed for The Great Exhibition, which was held in London's Hyde Park in 1851.

1919
Monument to the Third International
Vladimir Tatlin

The Monument to the Third International was designed to celebrate Russia's Third Communist International in 1919. It was to be composed of three glass volumes that would house offices and assembly halls, and these volumes were to move at different speeds. It was a visionary structure, but one that was never realised.

1929
Barcelona Pavilion
Ludwig Mies van der Rohe

The Barcelona Pavilion was created to showcase German design for the 1929 International Exposition, which was held in Barcelona, Spain. It questioned ideas of walls, floors and roof and introduced an architecture of planes. The Barcelona Pavilion represents a reductive approach to architectural forms.

1971–1977
Pompidou Centre
Richard Rogers and Renzo Piano

This building reinvents conventional ideas of service area (such as lifts and stairs) placement. Instead of being hidden in the depths of the building they are celebrated on the elevations. The Pompidou's frame is expressed on the outside of the building, liberating itself from the rest of the architecture.

1987
L'Institut du Monde Arabe
Jean Nouvel Architects

This building's glazed elevation uses a decorative mechanised screen to modify the light coming in to it. The building brings together traditional methods of screening and separation with sophisticated technology producing an elevation that adapts to varying external light levels to modify the interior environment.

1988–1992
Torre de Collserola
Foster + Partners

The Torre de Collserola is a 288-metre-high telecommunications tower, providing all-round views across Barcelona. The building is wrapped in glass to allow the all-round views, but also houses a structural glass platform on one of the decks. Using glass as a floor plate creates an even greater sense of excitement about both the building's interior and exterior views.

1931
Maison de Verre
Pierre Chareau

Literally translated, the 'house of glass' was designed in a traditional Parisian courtyard as an infill project. Maison de Verre uses ideas borrowed from industrial design including glass bricks and opening windows and shutters. This house is defined by light, which is transformed as it enters the building by the structure's glass block bricks.

1951
Farnsworth House
Ludwig Mies van der Rohe

At both its simplest and most complex this building has been reduced to a frame that is filled with glass. The Farnsworth House, in Illinois, USA, is a great example of steel and glass working in perfect harmony.

1958
Seagram Building
Ludwig Mies van der Rohe

The completion of this 38-storey building in 1958 suggested a new paradigm in architecture. Its reinforced concrete frame is wrapped with non-structural, bronze-tinted glass.

1989
Louvre Pyramid
IM Pei

The Louvre in Paris was reinvented by the architecture of IM Pei. He used a platonic shape – a pyramid made of glass – to make a connection between the museum and La Défense (an office development on the edge of Paris). Pei's pyramid is both architectural and culturally significant to Paris.

2003
Laban Dance Centre
Herzog & de Meuron

Glass is used in this building as a wrapping that mediates between inside and outside. The wrapping comprises a glass layer and an external outer polycarbonate skin, creating thermal and acoustic separation. This building plays with ideas of transparency, translucency and shadow.

2004
Swiss Re
Foster + Partners

This building, which uses glass as a skin and steel as a means to a liberated form, is a paradigm of the 21st century. It represents architecture of the future, incorporating aspects of environmental design with structural elegance.

Timeline: glass and steel › Origins and chronology

Experts believe that the ancient Syrians discovered glass-making, probably by accident, around 3000 BC. Syrian glass was a simple melted mixture of soda ash, lime and sand.

Historically, the application of glass in architecture has been limited by the manufacturing techniques used to produce it, as these controlled size of panels or pieces made. Its fragility has also made it expensive to produce, transport and handle. Advances in manufacturing and construction technologies, however, have allowed glass to be used in innovative applications and for structural purposes in contemporary architecture.

Spirituality and wealth

In places of worship numerous and large glass windows allow a building's interior to flood with light, which might suggest qualities of the heavenly and the divine. Medieval cathedrals used stained glass (the staining was achieved by painting or adding colours during the manufacturing process) to illuminate heavy cold spaces and create dramatic contrast in the interior. One of the most remarkable examples of this style is Chartres Cathedral (in Chartres, France), which has magnificent glazing dating from 1150. The colours of the cathedral's stained glass animate the interior and depict narrative scenes from the old and new testaments of the Bible.

In Elizabethan times glass was a rarity and its production a craft; as such its application in architecture was a good indicator of the wealth of a building's owner or occupant. Robert Smythson's Hardwick Hall (1591–1597) is one of the most significant country homes in England. Almost 40 per cent of its elevation is glazing. For the period, the use of so much glass was both rare and extravagant and led the building to be described as 'more glass than wall' by one commentator.

In the Georgian era, windows in buildings became larger to allow increased light and ventilation into the interior spaces. Their increased size made them heavier and more difficult to open and this led to the the introduction of the sliding sash window. The sash window could span large apertures and be opened easily using counterweights.

Glass and steel

Project: Kirche am Steinhof
Title: View of the stained glass
windows in the nave
Location: Vienna, Austria
Architect: Otto Wagner
Date: 1907

The Kirche am Steinhof (also called
the Church of St Leopold) in Vienna
is one of the most famous art
nouveau churches in the world.
Its mosaics and stained glass were
designed by Koloman Moser.

Protection and industry

During the Victorian era glass was used experimentally in horticulture to provide protection from harsh climates for plants, fruits and vegetables. This led to innovative designs for orangeries (glazed structures designed specifically to protect oranges) and greenhouses across northern Europe.

A pivotal point in contemporary architectural design and glass and steel construction technology was the realisation of Joseph Paxton's Crystal Palace. It was erected in London's Hyde Park to house the Great Exhibition of 1851 and brought together innovation in materials, construction and manufacturing. Paxton's Crystal Palace represents one of the earliest examples of a temporary, prefabricated structure and it was to influence and inform the design of many more vast industrial buildings, from market halls to railway stations, which needed to shelter large, open spaces and simultaneously allow lots of daylight to flood in. Cast iron columns and modular glazing systems created a new, functionally driven architectural language.

Project: Seagram Building
Location: New York, USA
Architect: Ludwig Mies van der Rohe
Date: 1958

The Seagram Building is 157 metres high and has 38 storeys. Its framework is steel from which non-structural glass walls are hung. Mies van der Rohe would have preferred for the steel frame to be left exposed; however, American building codes required that all structural steel be covered in a fireproof material. Concrete would have hidden the building's frame so Mies van der Rohe used non-structural bronze-toned I-beams to suggest structure instead. These beams are visible from the outside of the building and run vertically, surrounding the large glass windows.

Further experimentation in the use of glass in architecture is evident in Ludwig Mies van der Rohe's Barcelona Pavilion (1929). In this structure all walls, the floor and roof become planes and all standard conventions, such as the distinction between the horizontal and vertical or the inside and outside, are questioned. The pavilion's structural frame liberated the wall plane from its primarily load-bearing purpose. In Mies van der Rohe's vision the wall panel could be used primarily to separate interior and exterior spaces. Specifying glass for the purpose of building a wall thus became a real possibility.

In contemporary architecture, new buildings in our cities are ever taller and frequently approach the inconceivable. From Chicago's Home Insurance Building (which was completed in 1885 and is widely believed to be the world's first 'skyscraper'), to Taiwan's 509-metre high Taipei 101 building, all have been made possible by the technological advances made in steel and glass production.

When architects respond to a building brief, context is a primary consideration. This may describe a building's site, or it may refer to the cultural context of the surrounding environment. Steel and glass architecture has evolved dramatically from its 19th-century origins to the incredible heights of today's skyscraping possibilities, but throughout it has always been considered an architecture of the future.

The zeitgeist

Metals can be worked in many ways and this responds to their various industrial production processes, from casting and pressing to forging and extruding. Historically, architects and engineers who understood the potential of these processes (and the materials they produced) used this to create ideas and concepts that were strongly connected to a particular cultural idea. Art Nouveau architecture, for example, related to ideas of organic form and expression. Championed by Victor Horta and others, this expression was connected to artistic and cultural ideals that were popular in Belgium and France during the late 19th century (an example of these can be found in the designs for the Paris Metro entrances).

As an understanding of the potential of industrial materials developed, so too did the architecture that utilised them. Iron structures challenged architectural convention in the mid 19th century and liberated space, facilitating the largest buildings of their time.

Designed by Ferdinand Dutert and engineered by Victor Contamin, the Palais des Machines in Paris is perhaps the most important metal and glass building of the 19th century. It was an iron frame structure and, along with the Eiffel Tower, dominated the city's Exposition Universelle in 1889. The Palais des Machines had a span of 115 metres and length of 240 metres, but was dismantled in 1910. (The Eiffel Tower, however, used the same construction techniques and that it still exists is a testimony to that period of industrialisation of materials and structure.)

Project: L'Institut du Monde Arabe
Location: Paris, France
Architect: Jean Nouvel Architects
Date: 1987

For the façade design of the L'Institut du Monde Arabe, Jean Nouvel took the design of a traditional Islamic screen and used this as a means to modify the light entering the building. The glass and steel screen opens and closes depending on the surrounding light levels, which moderates the interior and exterior of the building. Nouvel's screen innovatively combines traditional design and contemporary technology to create a dynamic building that responds to its surrounding climatic conditions.

Material association

Glass (and steel) can be used to create impressive, functional and highly engineered architectural forms, and these forms can also suggest ideological issues via the construction materials used.

Glass offers the architect the potential to create building forms that can be immediately associated with the properties of the material itself, producing structures that are transparent, light, open and clear. For example, The Federal Parliament in Bonn, Germany (designed by Behnisch and Partners and completed in 1991) is one the first designs to use this powerful association in a contemporary parliament building (and was followed by Enric Miralles' Holyrood Building in Edinburgh, and Sir Norman Foster's Reichstag Dome in Berlin and Senedd building in Cardiff). The connection between these buildings' materiality and the openness of the democratic processes they house is no coincidence.

Project: The British Museum Great Court
Location: London, UK
Architect: Foster + Partners
Date: 2000

To allow the British Museum's Great Court to be used by visitors in all weather conditions it was covered with an undulating glazed roof. The roof has no visible supports and instead it spans the court area as a self-supporting structure. The undulating, minimal steel latticework supports 3312 triangular glass panels, each one different in size and shape.

Origins and chronology › **Cultural and material context** › Application

As part of the modernist aesthetic, glass and steel have commonly been associated with one another. The combination of both materials brings both strength and delicacy to architecture; a steel frame can appear quite 'light' and slender when combined with the transparency of a glass wall. Initially, glass and steel were used in particular for large, open-plan, industrial architectural applications, but advances in material technology have generated a greater range of possibilities for the use of both materials.

Structure and finishes

For the architect, one of the most important properties and key advantages of specifying the use of glass is its transparency: it allows light into a space. The limiting factors will be the weight and size of the glass pieces, as these could restrict both manufacture and transport to site.

The use of glass in building design need no longer be restricted to windows – it can also be used structurally too. Reinforced glazed pieces can be used as floor panels or stair treads and glazed structural columns (or fins) can be used to support glass walls. For example, the Apple store in New York, designed by Bohlin Cywinski Jackson, uses glass walls and structural elements to create a completely transparent architecture. Glass is also frequently used to construct curtain walls – non-load-bearing façades that are drawn across a building (much like a curtain) and attached to the front of the structure using specialist fixtures.

As well as structural uses, glass can be treated so that it can be applied as a finish, perhaps to create a decorative panel inside a building or to produce exterior cladding. A range of processes can alter the properties and appearance of glass. For example, it can be sandblasted, screen-printed or have materials applied to its surface to modify its opacity, or it may have layers of timber or metal applied to it to alter the way in which light interacts with the glass. Glass has become an important layer in the design process and manipulating it can change the experience of how light enters (or exits) a building or space, which can dramatically affect the whole architectural scheme.

Project: Selfridges store
Location: Birmingham, UK
Architect: Future Systems
Date: 2003

The organic form of this department store houses an enormous retail space and produces a completely inward-looking building. The building's outer skin is covered in thousands of aluminium discs, which create an impressive and distinctive architectural statement.

Glass and steel

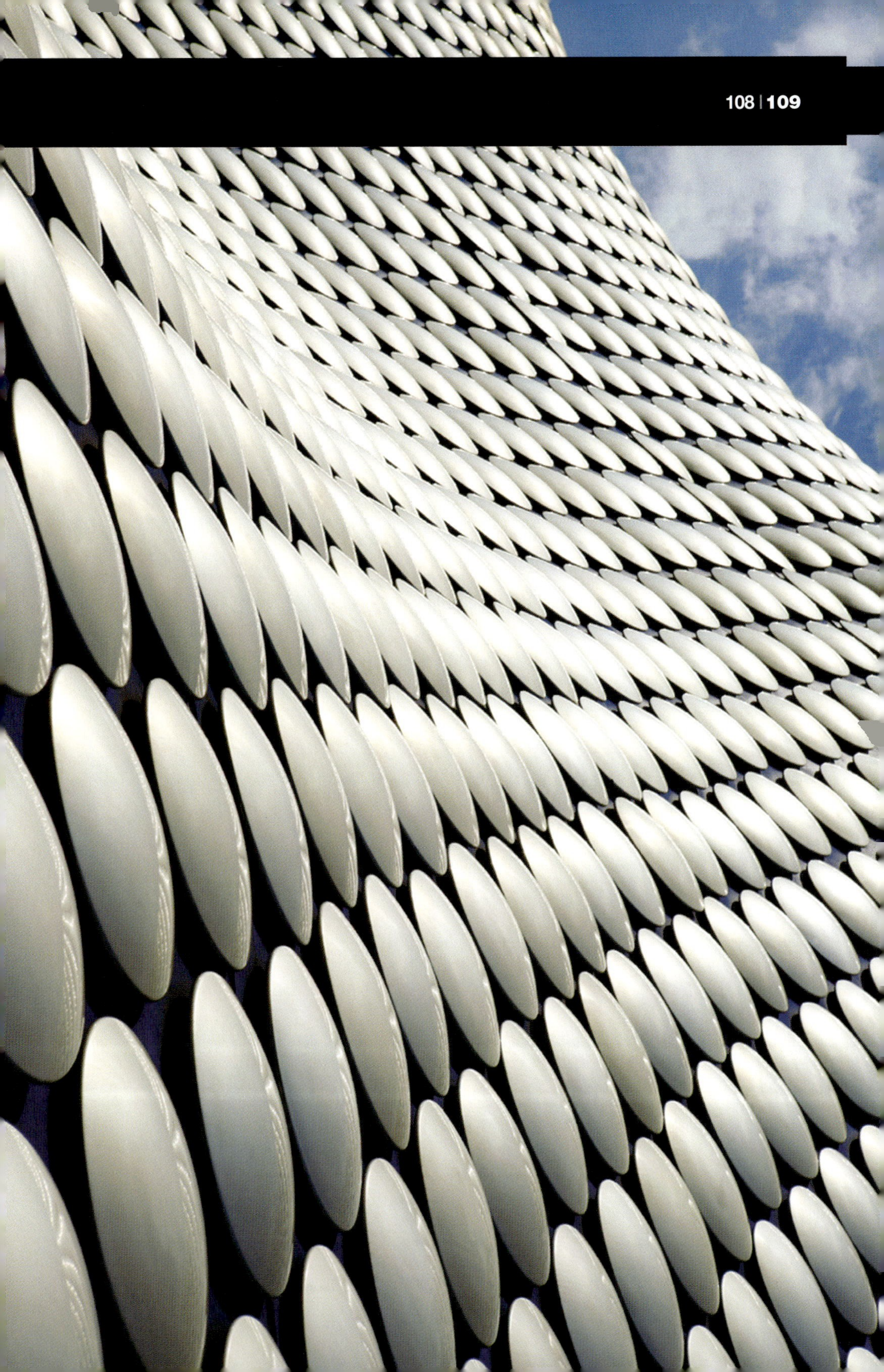

Project: The Kunsthaus Bregenz
Location: Bregenz, Austria
Architect: Peter Zumthor
Date: 1997

From the exterior, this building resembles a glass cube and at night it appears to glow. The Kunsthaus Bregenz is in fact a concrete structure that is encased in a glass façade. The glass panels are held within a steel frame, which is completely independent of the heavy, solid inner building. The glass is used to create impressive effects both internally and externally.

Surface treatments

Architects are increasingly exploring the ambiguities that different glass surface treatments can bring. Screen-printing dots or patterns on to the surface can suggest reflections when viewed from a distance and at close range allow shadows of the interior to be seen. Jean Nouvel, for example, has been experimenting with glass for over 20 years. He uses glass as a screen and prints on to its surface to provide separation from the substance of the building behind. In his architecture, glass surfaces act much like a veil.

Glass can also be treated with chemicals so that it is self-cleaning. This means it can be used in areas that may be difficult to access for maintenance. There are also surface treatments available that will reduce heat loss through the glass in the winter and control solar gain in the summer, allowing better temperature regulation.

Steel frames and finishes

The advantage that steel brings to architecture is its strength; a relatively slender steel structure can support numerous floor levels and, when combined with reinforced concrete, steel frames make ever taller structures achievable. The proposed super-tall Al Burj Dubai tower, for example, is intended to be over 1200 metres high and this prospect is only achievable by the structure's framework. Steel frames are often now visible on both the inside and outside of buildings as part of the expression of the architectural idea or concept.

Steel and other metal finishes are now an important consideration for the architect. William Van Alen's Chrysler Building (1928–1930), for example, is a classic example of how metal cladding can be used in construction to great effect.

Stainless steel has become a popular cladding material because it is durable, strong and can offer a variety of aesthetic effects, from highly reflective to 'flatter' surfaces. Aluminium cladding panels are lightweight and available in numerous colours, providing a variety of finishing possibilities for the architect. Core Ten is a type of steel that is intentionally weathered to produce a rusted appearance and is almost terracotta in colour. It is a popular cladding material because it provides a softer finish than stainless steel. Zinc is another cladding option and it can be covered in titanium to give a strong protective finish.

Metal can have different colours applied during its manufacturing process to produce decorative panels that may be used for cladding. A natural material that can achieve a similar effect is copper. Cladding panels made from copper or bronze will change from their original colour to an incredible green over time as the finish becomes **patinated**.

Patina
Patina is a coating of various chemical compounds such as oxides or carbonates that form on the surface of metal during exposure to weathering. The green patina that forms naturally on copper and bronze is known as verdigris and consists of copper carbonate. Artists and metalworkers often deliberately add patinas as a part of the original design and decoration of art and furniture, or to simulate antiquity in newly made objects.

Cultural and material context › Application › Grand master: Ludwig Mies van der Rohe

Ludwig Mies van der Rohe

German architect Ludwig Mies van der Rohe (1886–1969) transformed building design by challenging convention and embracing modern materials. Mies van der Rohe was a pioneer of 20th-century architecture and has had a profound effect on much contemporary architectural design and material application.

Mies van der Rohe was both an architect and an educator (he was architect director of the Bauhaus between 1930 and 1933). His holistic approach to design was not only evident in his building schemes, but also in his furniture designs (such as the Brno and Barcelona chairs). His architecture synthesised function, space, materials and structure and was characterised by the use of modern materials to define austere but elegant spaces. He developed the use of exposed steel frames and used glass to enclose and define space, striving for an architecture with a minimal framework of structural order.

Mies van der Rohe was interested in architecture of structural integrity and material honesty. His famous aphorism 'less is more' connects with the concept of architectural necessity; anything superfluous simply couldn't be justified. This concept developed into a rational approach that was reflected in the organisation, planning and detailing of his buildings.

The success of this reductive form of architecture was dependent on the material details: their aesthetics, properties and how they fitted together. Careful consideration of these created both the subtlety and the elegance of his architectural solutions.

Glass and steel

An exterior view of Mies van de Rohe's Barcelona Pavilion

The pavilion's interior frames the views to the outside

The Barcelona Pavilion

In 1929 Mies van der Rohe designed the Barcelona Pavilion. It was designed to showcase German innovation and was the country's entry for the 1929 International Exposition (which was held in Barcelona, hence the building's name).

The building represents an important milestone in the history of modern architecture as it used materials such as glass, marble and travertine to great effect. The pavilion stands on a large podium and the structure consists of eight steel posts that are cruciform in section and left exposed as part of the architectural language of the building. The steel posts support a flat roof (which is a plane of reinforced concrete), and the wall planes are either curtain glass or partition forms.

Central to the pavilion is an internal core slab of polished onyx, the dimensions of which affect the proportion and size of the building (the pavilion is twice the width and twice the length of the slab). The floor material is made from Roman travertine, and this is also used for the enclosing wall of the building's pool and office. The pavilion's sculpture pool is surrounded by green marble, and different coloured glass is used for the building's various screens.

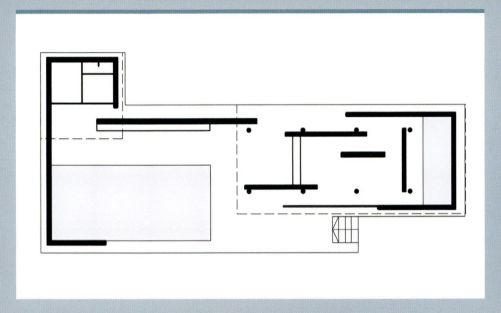

The Barcelona Pavilion's floor plan

The Barcelona Pavilion is an experiment in material application, structure and finish. It used materials and explored structure in ways that (prior to 1929) had not been imagined. It also challenged preconceived ideas of architectural form and posed questions about what defines the outside from the inside and what distinguishes a wall, roof or floor plane. In the Barcelona Pavilion, the floor planes and roof plane were horizontal surfaces and the walls were vertical slabs of glass or marble.

Mies van der Rohe used a limited palette of materials in his pavilion scheme, but each was carefully placed and considered to create an architecture that was both minimal and distinctive. His most famous pieces of furniture, the Barcelona chair and stool, were designed to complement the building. The pavilion was dismantled after the exhibition, but a replica was reconstructed in Barcelona in 1983.

The pavilion's columns are
expressed separately from
the walls

Glass and steel

Significant projects

1907	Riehl House, Potsdam, Germany
1911	Peris House, Zehlendorf, Germany
1913	Werner House, Zehlendorf, Germany
1917	Urbig House, Potsdam, Germany
1922	Kempner House, Charlottenburg, Germany
1922	Eichstaedt House, Wannsee, Germany
1922	Feldmann House, Wilmersdorf, Germany
1929	Barcelona Pavilion, Barcelona, Spain
1930	Tugendhat House, Brno, Germany
1951	Lake Shore Drive Apartments, Chicago, USA
1951	Farnsworth House, Plano, USA
1956	Crown Hall (College of Architecture at Illinois Institute of Technology), Illinois, USA
1958	Seagram Building, New York City, USA
1963	Lafayette Park, Detroit, USA
1968	New National Gallery, Berlin, Germany

Application › Grand master: Ludwig Mies van der Rohe › The McLaren Technology Centre

Foster + Partners | The McLaren Technology Centre

'As architects, my colleagues and I had been engaged for many years in meeting the challenge of social, technological and lifestyle change, the way they interlock and looking at the re-evaluation of the workplace as a good place to be. This inspiration has permeated down into the building itself.'
Sir Norman Foster

Glass and steel

The McLaren Technology Centre is the corporate and manufacturing headquarters for the McLaren Group. Designed by Foster + Partners, the group's state-of-the-art centre is located in Surrey, England. Foster + Partners are renowned internationally for their approach, which combines functional architectural design with an elegance in engineering. This combination produces expressive buildings that envelop and contain function, but challenge preconceptions of space via the innovative use of building materials.

The design brief

The McLaren headquarters fits the paradigm of a Foster + Partners building. McLaren depends on the continued development of high technology in order to produce some of the fastest Formula One cars in the world. The architecture that would become the company's headquarters needed to reflect this technological sophistication and serve as a 'laboratory' for McLaren's innovation.

McLaren came to the architects with a number of preconceptions, not about what the architecture should look like, but what the spirit of the building, its aspirations and its social generators should be.

An exterior view of the McLaren headquarters

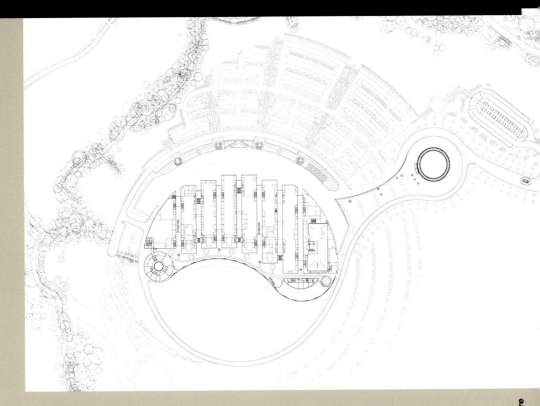

The building's site plan shows the scheme within its context, surrounded by a lake and carefully organised planting

Foster + Partners were asked to ensure that the headquarters would house the majority of the McLaren Group's employees (who had been previously scattered across 18 locations in Surrey). The architects worked with the client to respond to their working methodology and processes to ensure that the building could accommodate their experimental, developmental and manufacturing needs.

There was a natural synergy between McLaren and Foster+ Partners and in determining what the architect and client, both of whom came from very different design disciplines, wanted to achieve.

Grand master: Ludwig Mies van der Rohe › The McLaren Technology Centre

The design solution

The McLaren Technology Centre uses high-specification steel and glass to suggest a 'future' architecture in terms of material development and design.

The centre's semi-circular plan is completed by a formal lake, which forms an integral part of the building's cooling system. The principal lakeside façade is a continuous curved glass wall that looks out across the landscape and is shaded by a cantilevered roof.

The centre is constructed on an in-situ concrete slab that was cut into the landscape to keep the height of the building below a set restriction of 11 metres above ground level. The deep-plan building was sunk into the landscape and shielded from view by the planting of 100,000 specially selected new trees and ornamental shrubs.

Glass and steel

The centre's interior offers views across the landscape

The building's framework is a steel skeleton wrapped in a skin of glass and aluminium cladding, which creates a strong character for both the interior and exterior shells. The main body of the centre is broken into 18-metre-wide 'fingers', with six-metre wide strips (or 'streets') between them. The streets allow daylight into the building, give those working inside it an awareness of the outside and form a central part of the centre's ventilation system. In cross section, 18-metre-wide mezzanine floors are incorporated from ground to roof level.

The design of the centre's interior responds directly to the building's highly detailed and finished exterior. All the interior furnishings specified complement the clean and efficient working environment. Floor-to-ceiling glazed panels ensure a strong visual connection between the interior of building and its surrounding landscape and ecosystem and this theme is enforced by the incorporation of eye-level, abstract art works that are housed in glazed panels and placed around individual workstations.

There are five lakes at the McLaren Technology Centre: the formal lake at the front of the building and a further series of interconnected ecology lakes. The lakes are functional as well as aesthetically pleasing and their 50,000 cubic metres of water form a vital part of the building's cooling infrastructure. Water is pumped – one third directly and two thirds via a natural filtration system of reed beds and a cleansing biotope – through a series of heat exchangers that extract heat from the chiller plant.

The water is recirculated via a 160-metre-long cascade that extends around the far edge of the lake. The water's temperature reduces as it cascades down a series of shallow steps and its fast-flowing movement causes it to aerate, thereby helping to oxygenate the system.

The creation of this functionally designed working environment has been given the same careful consideration as a beautifully engineered machine might; materials have been tested and specified and construction details executed with precision. The result is the creation of a 'complete' environment, both inside and out.

One of the centre's 'streets'

Grand master: Ludwig Mies van der Rohe ⟩ The McLaren Technology Centre

The glass cladding incorporates a thin veneer of marble, which lends a translucent quality to the gallery's façade

The building's curved roof sweeps the façade down onto the street

Founded in 1980 by Sir Nicholas Grimshaw, Grimshaw Architects is responsible for a number of critically acclaimed projects. The architecture of this practice has long been defined by originality, in terms of its design, material application and engineering. The architecture of the practice characteristically responds to the potential of the construction material specified, whether this is glass, steel or a composite material.

The practice is also renowned for its design process, in particular its unique modelling approach. This approach has allowed Grimshaw Architects to design environments that are both sensitive and sustainable. The tubular steel-frame and thermoplastic ETFE-clad biomes of Cornwall's Eden Project are one such example of this. Here, Grimshaw's architectural response uses innovative materials and design approaches to create a completely enclosed and controlled environment. Another example is the Fundación Caixa Galicia, in the province of Galicia, Spain.

The design brief

Grimshaw's first design scheme for an art and cultural centre is dedicated to the collection of Spanish financial institution Fundación Caixa Galicia. As well as providing suitable space to house its pieces, the client sought an inviting civic building that would draw public visitors inside and also offer exclusive facilities for private functions. Another key aspect of the design brief was to ensure that the response was sensitive to the site, which is located in the historic city of A Coruña, north-west Spain.

'I am strongly of the belief that one always ought to try to design in the age you live in with the materials of the age you live in... Up to the early part of this [the twentieth] century, there were no controls on fitting in, people just simply did the best thing they could with the materials of their age and that's why I think the buildings have a certain kind of credibility and people accept them for being good buildings.'
Sir Nicholas Grimshaw

Glass and steel

The building's floor plan

The design solution

The 5500m^2 Fundación Caixa Galicia arts centre is located in the historic quarter of A Coruña and occupies the last 'gap' on a street of glazed balconies, which have become emblematic of the old town. Grimshaw's designs for both the existing and new buildings needed to be sensitive to the distinctive architecture of its neighbours and conform to the dictates of the existing building regulations (particularly in regard to building height).

It required an imaginative response to provide a smooth graduation from the building's soaring front elevation (overlooking the port), to the lower-lying administrative building that adjoins the site at the rear. As well as making this transition, the new building had to establish a dialogue between historical and contemporary design.

The solution that emerged is a tilted paraboloid. The form's apex peaks at the front elevation, before falling steeply down the street façade on an inverse incline and plunging below ground level. The gallery's street-facing elevation is clad with glass panelling that incorporates a slender marble interlayer. This translucent skin provides the building with a rich luminosity and allows daylight to permeate the gallery. In darkness, it allows the building to appear softly illuminated.

The building comprises seven floors of superstructure and four basement levels, and features a glazed internal 'street', glass bridges, inclined panoramic elevators, column-free exhibition galleries and a 300-seat auditorium.

The gallery has been described as a building of contradictions: open yet closed; connected yet clearly divided; and public but with carefully secluded private spaces. It is perhaps the full-height atrium that creates these tensions. It spans the longitudinal section of the building and forms the backbone of the gallery's circulation. The glazed atrium visually and physically 'slices' the building in section and allows daylight to flood the visitor's vertical circulation path (which is a prominent staircase that creates a sculptural presence in the central atrium void). The use of glass throughout ensures that daylight is optimised wherever possible. Where artificial lighting is relied upon, it is set into the fabric of the building to create unobtrusive illumination.

The building's below-ground levels are housed in a granite base and this heavy, timeless material anchors the structure. The paving slabs used on the ground floor are also granite, echoing the street paving and providing a connection between the architecture and its external surroundings.

The specification and use of materials on this build, from the glass wall on the exterior form to the interior's white plaster finish, suggests a lightness and openness, imbuing a sense of both transparency and accessibility.

Materials can be classified in many different ways. Some are found or extracted from the earth (such as stone or timber) and some are manufactured from natural components (such as glass and steel). Composite materials are those that are designed and produced from a range of other resources (natural, synthetic or man-made) to perform a particular function.

The properties of composite materials can be engineered to respond to particular design conditions; for example they may be especially durable, strong or waterproof depending on the requirements of the build. The key advantage of using composite materials in architectural design is that they are hugely flexible: by varying their composition and constituent parts different solutions for different projects can be found.

Importantly the range of materials in this category can grow from an understanding of material application in other areas of industry. This sort of innovation occurs as scientists, engineers, architects and designers respond to one another's work, begin to think outside the realms of their specialist fields and creatively apply composite materials across different disciplines.

The possibilities for this material group are ever growing. Our natural resources are in limited supply and composite materials will become increasingly important in order to reduce the amount of 'raw' materials that are used in architectural design.

Project: MK Forty Tower
Location: Milton Keynes, UK
Architects: dRMM
Date: 2007

In 2007 Milton Keynes Gallery (MKG) invited dRMM to design a temporary pavilion to mark the 40th anniversary of the city of Milton Keynes. dRMM proposed a tower to conceptually contrast with the predominant horizontality of the city. The freestanding pavilion is made of cross-laminated prefabricated sections of MDF timber. The MK Forty tower is 19 metres high; visitors can climb 101 wooden steps to reach a platform with panoramic views of the city and the landscape beyond.

1986
Lloyds Building
Richard Rogers Partnership

This building has a machine-like appearance and is made of prefabricated elements that 'lock' together. The Lloyds building reinvented the idea of construction; its service areas (such as stairs, lifts and toilets) are located at the edge of the building freeing the central space for office use.

1997
Eberswalde Technical Library
Herzog & de Meuron

The Eberswalde library was designed in collaboration with artist Thomas Ruff. The building's form is a simple cube sheathed in glass and cast-concrete panels that are arranged in horizontal bands. Each band shows a single image, which is repeated 66 times, producing a static film strip.

1997
Guggenheim Museum
Frank Gehry

Located in Bilbao, Spain, the most distinctive and remarkable aspects of this building are its shape and its material application. Its sculptural dynamic shape is only possible because titanium, the material used for the building's cladding panels, is incredibly flexible.

2003
Selfridges store
Future Systems

The skin of this Birmingham department store is clothed in thousands of aluminium discs. These cover the entire surface of the building, creating a 'chain-mail' aesthetic and producing an organic, light-reflecting effect.

2003
Kunsthaus
Peter Cook and Colin Fournier

This art museum has become an architectural landmark in Graz, Austria. An example of 'blob' architecture, it is distinctive in form and colour. Its formwork is a reinforced concrete box that is covered in blue plastic, creating an organic shape. At night the museum is carefully illuminated to exaggerate the unusual shape.

2003
Lagotronics Headquarters

Located in Venlo, The Netherlands, the façade of the Lagotronics headquarters incorporates 72 acrylic panels that light up a surface area of nearly 165 square metres. Amazingly transparent, the whole construction allows light to enter the building during the day but reveals a chase of differently coloured squares at night.

2000
The 02 Arena
Richard Rogers Partnership

London's O2 Arena (the 'Dome') is covered by a polytetrafluoroethylene (PTFE) plastic roof. The space within it is 50 metres high and the roof is supported by a series of masts and cables. The building has taken its popular name from its defining feature, its roof structure.

2000
Japanese Pavilion
Shigeru Ban

Shigeru Ban is famous for his innovative structures created from paper, particularly recycled cardboard tubes. Ban created the Japanese Pavilion at Expo 2000 in Hanover, Germany. The 72-metre-long gridshell structure was made with paper tubes. After the exhibition the structure was recycled and returned to paper pulp.

2001
Eden Project
Grimshaw Architects

The Eden Project features a series of glazed biomes (climatically controlled environments containing ecosystems). The biomes are made from a tubular steel frame that contains hexagonal panels of ethylene tetrafluoroethylene (ETFE), a type of plastic that is designed to have high strength and thermal resistance.

2004
Galleria shopping centre
UNStudio

Located in Seoul, Korea, the façade of the Galleria shopping centre projects an ever-changing surface. In total, 4330 glass discs are mounted on the concrete skin of the building. The discs include special dichroic foil, generating a mother-of-pearl effect during the day. At night each glass disc is lit by LED lights, which are programmed to create a multitude of aesthetic effects.

2006
Water Cube
Arup and PTW Architects

Beijing's National Aquatics Centre was constructed to house water events for the 2008 Olympic Games. The 'Cube's' main structure is made of concrete and steel and the form is clad with ETFE plastic, which is moulded to resemble bubbles. The material is transparent and fills the space with light.

2006
Stripe Theatre
Design Engine Architects

This building is clad with Prodema. Prodema is made from heat-hardened synthetic-resin-bonded cellulose fibre. It has a neutral wood surface and a protective lining. Prodema appears to have a natural finish, but it is much more durable than naturally sourced materials.

Timeline: composite materials › Origins and chronology

Project: Serpentine Gallery Pavilion
Location: London, UK
Architect: Frank Gehry
Date: 2008

Frank Gehry's Serpentine Gallery
Pavilion is anchored by four huge
steel columns that support large
timber planks and a complex
network of overlapping glass
planes, which create a dramatic,
multi-dimensional space.

Composite materials are not classified as 'pure' in either
their composition or application. These materials have
been adapted from their original form to create
engineered hybrids that can serve multiple functions
in building design. For example, materials that combine
the aesthetic qualities of wood with the durability of
plastic are now available thanks to advances in material
science and technology.

If they are to inform architecture, understanding the
properties of these materials is essential and requires
architects, engineers and designers to collaborate with
product manufacturers. Doing so will allow designers to
respond to the range of possibilities that such materials can
bring to architectural design and the construction process.

Plastics

The 20th century saw new industrial and chemical processes
used to create a range of composite materials. The earliest of
these were plastics (created in 1885).

Plastic materials are collectively known as polymers.
A polymer has a molecular structure that is built up from
a number of similar units, which are all bonded together.
The term refers to a range of materials including plastic and
synthetic resin. 'Plastic' is also a generic term that describes
a material quality, something that can transform to take on
new shapes and be moulded into different forms.

One of the earliest and most influential synthetic materials
was Bakelite. Invented in 1907 by Leo Hendrik Baekeland,
Bakelite was used extensively for all sorts of products from
telephones to light switches.

In 1938 Roy Plunkett developed polytetrafluoroethylene
(PTFE) or **Teflon** for use as a protective coating (it was used
in the manufacture of the atomic bomb). A contemporary
example of PTFE's architectural application can be found in
the structural fabric roof of London's O2 Arena.

Glass-reinforced plastic (GRP) uses glass fibre as a structural
element and this is bonded with epoxy resins. GRP is a
strong, lightweight material that has low thermal conductivity.
It was first used in aircraft manufacturing in the 1940s and in
boat building in the 1950s.

Ethylene tetrafluoroethylene (ETFE) is a type of plastic that is lightweight and transparent and is commonly used in large-span structures that require lots of natural light. Recently, ETFE has been used in the construction of the Eden Project in Cornwall, England, and the National Aquatics Centre in Beijing, China.

Carbon fibre

Carbon fibre is the basis of most carbon structures. It was first manufactured in 1958 and is made from thousands of thin carbon strands that are tightly twisted together. Carbon fibre was commonly used as a manufacturing material in the aircraft industry as it is both strong and lightweight. In construction it is often used to create structural frames as it is stronger than steel, but a great deal lighter.

The future of composite materials in construction is bright. As material technology allows us to better understand their potential, the application of composite materials in new contexts is growing. Many of these materials find their origins in areas outside of architecture and construction, but inventive thinking and cross-discipline collaboration is bringing them into the world of building design.

Teflon

Teflon (or polytetrafluoroethylene) is a non-stick coating that is commonly found in a range of different applications, from saucepans and clothing to body armour and computer components. Its use was developed and popularised by American chemical company, DuPont. In architecture and construction, PTFE coatings are often applied to materials to make them more durable.

Project: The Beijing National Stadium
Location: Beijing, China
Architect: Herzog & de Meuron (and Ai Weiwei)
Date: 2008

Also known as the 'bird's nest', Beijing's National Stadium is the largest steel structure in the world. The steel structure is clearly visible on the outside of the building and also provides a distinctive frame for the stadium. Its woven-like structure is suggestive of a bird's nest, hence the name.

Project: East Beach Café
Location: West Sussex, UK
Architect: Thomas Heatherwick
Date: 2007

The East Beach Café is a south-facing single-storey building located on the Sussex coast. Its exposed seaside location will subject the building to heavy weathering, with the high salt content of the air speeding the natural degradation of all materials. With this in mind, Thomas Heatherwick opted for naturally finished materials that respond well to the local environment. The steel shell that forms the building's outer skin will rust and gain character as it ages, while an oil-based coating applied after the surface has 'weathered' will help to prolong the life of the building.

Synthetic materials are a modern phenomenon. Informed by the changing nature of manufacture, the 20th century saw great innovation in material science. In particular, this period saw the automobile, aeronautical and space industries develop complex materials that would later be used in the construction industry.

Appropriation and substitution

For example, in the 1930s, DuPont created Neoprene. Neoprene (originally called Duprene) was the first mass-produced synthetic rubber compound. It was (and still is) used in a wide variety of products, such as wetsuits, electrical insulation and fan belts for cars. Neoprene is both waterproof and fire-resistant and, as such, it was appropriated by architecture for use as window and door seals and for gaskets in cladding systems.

As well as the sophisticated, multiple functionality they can offer, composite materials are often specified by architects as a substitute for costly natural materials. Polycarbonates, for example, are thermoplastic polymers that can be easily worked and moulded; they are temperature- and impact-resistant and can create a lightweight and transparent material. The properties of polycarbonates make them a lighter, easier to instal and cheaper alternative to the use of glass in architectural design.

Composite materials

A sustainable future?

A key consideration for the use of composite materials in architecture today is that synthetic polymers are composed of (mostly) non-renewable resources (such as crude oil). In contrast, natural polymers are made from plants and renewable resources. Looking to the future, synthetic materials must evolve so that they respond to new contexts and consumer demands. With limited natural resources, our synthetic materials need to be incorporated in architectural designs in such a way that they can be removed and reused for alternative applications on other projects. They also need to be increasingly durable so as to reduce waste over longer periods of time.

The evolution of composite materials is a critical part of the design palette for our future buildings. With foresight, we can engineer these materials so that their properties and functionality suits contemporary lifestyles and living environments. Crucially, architects and designers must ensure a continued understanding of material application in other design industries so that they can continue to innovate.

Project: The Eden Project
Location: Cornwall, England
Architect: Grimshaw Architects
Date: 2001

The Eden project comprises a series of managed climatic environments (or biomes) that are housed underneath a dome-like structure. These domes are made from a tubular steel space frame that allows flexibility in both form and structure. This is clad in ethylene tetrafluoroethylene (ETFE), which can respond to high temperature ranges and allow light into the spaces.

The application of composite materials in architecture may range from small-scale use in window and door seals to vast cladding systems or prefabricated building panels. The very nature of composite materials means they can be manufactured to suit the conditions and requirements of the site or building context. The limitations for these materials are not related to their natural condition or found state (as would be the case with timber or stone), but instead are the methods of manufacture, transportation and installation.

Synthetic materials in architectural design tend to be used more for interior finishes and fixtures (for example, electrical, plumbing or lighting systems) than for structural purposes. They can also be used for exterior cladding systems, which can lend an interesting aesthetic to a building's exterior form. For example, polyvinyl chloride (PVC)-coated polyester fabric or polytetrafluoroethylene (PTFE)-coated glass fibre fabrics are commonly used to create **tensile** roofs on airport, warehouse and exhibition spaces because their properties make them very appropriate for covering large, open spaces.

A wide range of emerging materials have been specifically produced to deal with some of the issues facing contemporary architecture, including efficiency of construction and sustainable use of resources. The development of these materials will provide the architect with ever increasing possibilities.

Polycarbonate materials

Polycarbonate materials are used extensively in buildings (often where glass may have otherwise been used). They have exceptional transparency, high strength, resist ultraviolet radiation and can also cope with extremely high temperatures. Additionally they are lightweight, and so require much less structural support than glass (which if used in a similar context would be much heavier).

The 'appropriateness' of materials is a key consideration for architects in the design process. For example, the surface of polycarbonate materials can become scratched and over time this will reduce its transparency. As such, polycarbonate materials should only be used as a substitute for glass in conditions that are not exposed to extreme scratching.

Polytetrafluoroethylene (PTFE)

PTFE (also known as Teflon) is very tough and commonly used to surface coat other materials in order to strengthen or protect them. PTFE is dirt-resistant because its properties prevent other particles from sticking to its surface, so is useful in areas where maintenance or cleaning access to a building may be limited.

Polymethyl methylacrylate (PMMA)

PMMA (also known as acrylic) is a very hard material that is used to toughen various surfaces and also as an additive to finishes and paints. It is also used in place of glass for both interior and exterior conditions.

Polyvinyl chloride (PVC)

Often used as an alternative to timber or stone, PVC is utilised extensively in buildings to make drainpipes, plumbing fixings, doors or window frames and cladding systems. It is flexible, durable, requires little or no maintenance and can be easily fixed and replaced. It can also be incorporated in many interior applications and can offer prefabricated solutions for bathrooms, kitchens and furniture elements.

Tensile structures

A tensile structure is a construction element that only carries tension and no compression or bending. Most tensile structures need to be supported by some form of compression or bending component, such as masts (as is evident in the O2 Arena in London), compression rings or beams. Tensile membrane structures are most often used as roofs as they can economically and attractively span large distances.

Cultural and material context › Application › Grand master: Charles Eames

Charles Eames

American designers Charles and Ray Eames explored ideas in film, three-dimensional design, product design, furniture design, exhibition design and architecture. In 1929, Charles travelled across Europe and was heavily influenced by the aesthetics and principles of the modern movement. On his return, he and his wife, Ray, began to experiment with materials and were commissioned to design plywood leg splints for the US Navy. The knowledge they acquired during this process was later applied to their furniture design; the specifications for the iconic Eames chair (1956) incorporated a plywood shell.

The knowledge that Charles and Ray acquired from each of their projects was applied to successive design concepts and realisations. Once they had specified the use of fibreglass and aluminium in their furniture designs, for example, they transferred the same application to their architectural designs, appropriating the same material use from small-scale three-dimensional forms to the ultimate three-dimensional product.

Their approach to design was challenging, demanding and ground-breaking. It questioned, explored and deconstructed previous preconceptions and established schools of thought in order to identify new ways to apply materials and create both products and the spaces that they occupy.

Composite materials

The Eames House offers an innovative approach to architectural design

The distinctive façade of the
Eames House

**Section drawing of the
Eames House**

Case Study House No. 8 (The Eames House)

In the period following the Second World War, *California Arts
and Architecture* magazine launched an initiative to see how
modern manufacturing techniques might provide a solution
to America's post-war housing problems. The magazine's
Case Study House Program was designed to produce
architectural schemes that would accommodate the needs
and functions of a modern household, using contemporary
materials and construction processes. The magazine tracked
the progress of a number of case study homes, before,
during and after their construction. Charles and Ray Eames
designed Case Study House No. 8 (1945–1949). The house
remains on its site today in the Pacific Palisades, California.

In an attempt to re-employ workers and factories that had
supported the production of wartime armaments and aircraft,
the design of the Eames House responded to ideas of mass
production, composite parts and rapid assembly. Its design
scheme incorporated a steel-frame structure and
prefabricated windows and stairs, and proposed a sense
of material and structural economy; of maximising internal
space and creating an open living area. This was a revolution
in house design; traditionally a domestic abode was
segregated into spaces for living, food preparation and
sleeping. The Eames' design challenged this norm and
suggested a new way of living in and occupying a home.

Composite materials

The design of the Eames House was heavily influenced by the work of European modernists such as Mies van der Rohe and Le Corbusier. However, the pavilion structures designed by Mies van der Rohe (such as his Barcelona Pavilion, see pages 112–117) were minimal and abstract forms, but the Case Study homes were designed to be commercial and have broad appeal. To resolve this conflict, the building frame and materials of the Eames House were simple (in keeping with the modernist ideals), but its interior was designed in such a way that the American public could immediately connect with it.

This house was designed to work as a set of manufactured components. The main support for the house was a steel frame, which was fixed onto a concrete base. The walls were either glazed panels or timber panels (for the interior) and sliding screens provided separation and privacy for the sleeping areas as the main living space was double height.

The house was made available as a frame and panel system for the Herman Miller company (which remains an important furniture and design company today), and was sold as an off-the-shelf, ready-made design solution that promised a modern lifestyle in an easy-to-assemble, affordable kit.

Charles and Ray Eames were visionary in their ability to combine industrial technology and manufacturing processes with architectural design. Their scheme's simple exposed frame, plentiful open-plan space and modesty in its design have become significant influences on future generations of architects.

Significant events

1929   Charles Eames spends time in Europe and discovers the buildings of Ludwig Mies van der Rohe and Le Corbusier

1930   Opens an architectural office in St Louis, Missouri, with Charles Gray

1936   Designs the modern-style Meyer House in collaboration with Eliel Saarinen

1940   Collaborates with Eero Saarinen on cabinets and chairs for an Organic Design competition at MoMA, New York

1941   Marries Ray Kaiser

1942   The Eames open a design studio

1946   Designs the Eames Molded Plywood Lounge Chair

1948   Designs the La Chaise Chair with Eero Saarinen for MoMA, New York's Low-Cost Furniture Competition

1949   Designs the Case Study House No 8, Pacific Palisades, California

1950   Designs the (unbuilt) Billy Wilder House

1951   Designs the Wire Mesh Chair

1956   Designs the Lounge Chair, (which is manufactured by Herman Miller)

1964   Designs the IBM Pavilion at the New York World's Fair.

1968   *Power of Ten*, one of the Eames' most influential films, is produced

1978   Charles Eames dies

Application › Grand master: Charles Eames › House of Fraser, Bristol

'The practice's core aim is to inspire users through their experience of space, light and materials.'
Taken from the Stanton Williams website

Composite materials

The exterior of the House of Fraser
store in Bristol, UK

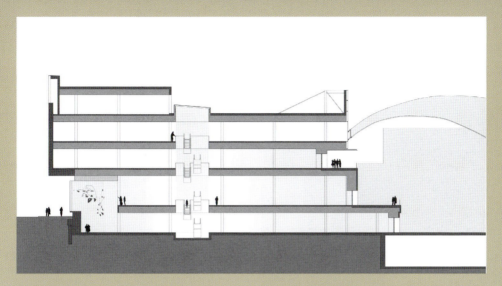

Stanton Williams Architects have a
reputation for sensitively engaging with
materials and space. The practice has
worked on a range of prestigious projects
in a number of historic sites including the
Tower of London, Compton Verney House
in Warwickshire and Whitby Abbey
in Yorkshire.

The latest projects in Stanton Williams'
portfolio respond to many of the issues
facing architecture today, such as
sustainable, energy-efficient buildings
and sensitivity to context, whether historic
or urban.

**Section drawing that shows how
light can penetrate the store's high
front windows**

The design brief

The project to design a flagship store
in Bristol city centre (south-west England)
offered Stanton Williams Architects a chance
to consider the idea that a department store
might form an important urban landmark.
The design brief created an opportunity for
SWA to produce a window across the city;
the prominence of this site meant that the
building's façade would have a great
presence in the city centre. As such the
design needed to be distinctive and offer
something different to the city.

The design solution

SWA's design for the House of Fraser
store in Bristol (2008) is not only distinctive
because of its scale (the store is 15,800
square metres over four floors), but also
because of the way in which it responds to
the site and its position within the context of
Bristol's city centre. Occupying a high-profile
position at the eastern tip of the site, it is the
very first building visible on approaching
Bristol's city centre.

Grand master: Charles Eames › House of Fraser, Bristol › The Kingsdale School

The façade used stone (top)
and bronze (above) **panels**

Stanton Williams have created a building of powerful visual interest. The building's façade was designed with the help of a range of artists and craftsmen, mixing traditional craft skills and new production techniques to produce an impressive and dramatic elevation.

This building challenges convention and champions architectural innovation. It has one of the largest display windows in Europe (a single-glazed 6 x 30-metre panel), which provides views into the building and allows the store to emanate a 'glow' at night. An important design consideration for any retail store is to provide adequate light levels: natural light floods this building via the enormous display window and also a central glazed atrium.

This building uses materials in an innovative way. The standard front-of-store large glass windows commonly associated with department stores were reinvented using specialised techniques; transforming the ordinary into the extraordinary.

The building's main elevation is clad with a combination of Portland stone (that is embedded with real fossils), bronze and glass panels. The stone was honed (rather than polished) to remove any visible surface saw marks made from cutting it.

Artist Susanna Heron transformed the façade into a work of art. Heron produced abstract interpretations of natural forms and used the textured surface of the Portland stone as inspiration for her glazed surface design. Her artwork was then transferred on to a vinyl mask, which was then applied to the glass panels. The panels were sandblasted and acid-etched to create a relief and provide texture to the surface area. When finished, the panels were attached to vertical steel fins using bolt fixings.

At the building's ground level the façade is clad with bronze panels. Each one is cast individually, producing a unique surface that has both smooth and highly textured areas. The bronze panels were cut with industrial drilling machines, which worked to add more texture to the surface and give it depth.

The House of Fraser store in Bristol represents a series of collaborations, between client, architect, artist and manufacturer. All parties were united by a vision to work creatively and apply an abstract idea of material and surface to a realised architectural form. This building succeeds, in large part, because of its façade, which has been beautifully crafted to create a showcase in contemporary design and innovation.

The stone and bronze panels technically and aesthetically complement one another

Grand master: Charles Eames › House of Fraser, Bristol › The Kingsdale School

An interior shot of the geodesic
dome auditorium

Alex de Rijke, Philip Marsh and Sadie Morgan founded dRMM, a London-based studio of international architects and designers, in 1995. The practice embraces projects that are innovative, high quality and socially useful. dRMM's projects are characteristically led by site and client needs, concept and construction. Each partner brings a range of skills to the practice, working from interior design to master planning and challenging conventional approaches to application of materials in practice and design.

The design brief

Originally built in the 1950s, the Kingsdale School suffered from narrow corridors, inadequate staff rooms and classrooms that were too hot in summer and too cold in winter. In 2004 dRMM was commissioned to remodel the Kingsdale School in Dulwich, London. The practice was asked to use architectural design to redefine the identity of this secondary state school and reinvent the way in which Kingsdale's staff and students could work and learn in the school's existing buildings. Specific requirements were that the building was phased to work with existing functions and that a large gathering space was created for performance, meetings and public community use.

The design solution

This design scheme challenges the conventions of what's expected of school buildings, seeking to positively inspire academic standards and the pride of a school community with radical architecture. The building itself is seen as a catalyst to inspire the school's children and teachers through their use of the building.

dRMM's redevelopment of the school is marked by the world's largest variable-skin ETFE roof, which covers an internal courtyard space. The roof is supported by the existing building, which means that no columns were needed, freeing up the space below. The roof's multi-layered skin acts as a 'pillowed' membrane that can be pumped with air on cool days to provide insulation and deflated on hot days to allow the courtyard to cool down.

The variable-skin ETFE enclosure creates a new kind of socially oriented education space. This flexible, mixed-use space provides new entry, circulation, dining, library and assembly areas under one roof. Aerial walkways connect stairs and reduce corridors. There is also a new staircase, lift and bridge within this space.

The courtyard is animated by a geodesic dome that houses an auditorium and library. The form of this three-dimensional, engineered-timber, prefabricated structure was made possible by the use of computer-controlled cutting machines. The dome's form consists of an asymmetrical geodesic softwood primary structure, with a sandwich panel acoustic secondary structure as finish. The auditorium can seat more than 300 people and is used for performances, presentations and meetings.

This scheme successfully achieves its goal of improving the school environment by means of a simple and bold strategy: covering the existing courtyard with a wide-span, translucent roof and replacing the old assembly hall with a new state-of-the-art auditorium. Modern materials and construction techniques have been utilised successfully to create a cutting-edge learning environment.

Composite materials

A section drawing of the school

The new courtyard space that
houses the school's auditorium

Architects have a responsibility to use materials intelligently and our future buildings will need to be designed using resources that are, as far as is possible, both efficient and renewable. In addition to considering the source of a material it is also increasingly necessary for the architect to explore the way in which materials can be innovatively utilised so as to make the resulting architecture sustainable. This could mean incorporating materials that make a building more thermally efficient (so that less non-sustainable fuel is required to heat it) or may require thinking about the ways in which materials, or even building structures, might be recycled or reused in a range of different contexts. The emergence and development of 'smart' materials, which respond to different stimuli, are also changing design possibilities for the architect.

The examples and concepts in this section are varied. Some are the result of the experimentation with development and appropriation of existing ideas and practices, while others are visionary, offering a glimpse at the potential for our buildings and spaces of the future.

Title: Detail of the
Guggenheim Museum
Location: Bilbao, Spain
Architect: Frank Gehry
Date: 1997

Like much of Gehry's other works, the steel-frame structure of the Guggenheim Museum consists of radically sculpted, organic contours. Its reflective titanium panels resemble fish scales or undulating waves, echoing the other organic life forms that recur commonly in Gehry's designs. Computer-Aided Three-Dimensional Interactive Application (CATIA) and visualisations were used heavily in the structure's design.

Innovation

Innovative forms

It's not just materials and concepts that can be innovative; a building's form can be too. For example, Frank Gehry uses materials that produce complex structures, allowing for a dynamic architecture (see pages 152 and 155).

Moulded forms

Materials that can be poured and shaped in moulds (such as concrete or plastic), taken to site and pieced together allow the architect to realise complex, dynamic and innovative forms and structures.

Material advances

Advances in material science can produce new and innovative possibilities. For example, Litracon is a building material that is composed of fine concrete and optical glass fibres. This creates a 'translucent' concrete, offering the architect an array of new application options.

Photomechanical materials

In architecture, photomechanical materials can be used to adjust ventilation systems or allow a building's skin to adopt a different shape or behaviour when exposed to different lighting conditions.

Touch-sensitive technology

This technology can be used in architectural design to allow interactivity between the user and their environment.

Adaptable environments

The future will see the creation of buildings and spaces that can adapt to the various needs of their users. Spaces that can be used flexibly, either by moving walls or altering the spatial configuration, offer an innovative approach.

Remote control

Buildings of the near future could be controlled via mobile phone technology, allowing devices such as heating systems to be switched on and off remotely. There is also likely to be an increasingly strong relationship between communication technology and building environments.

Microarchitecture

Designs for 'micro' spaces that can be used for living, working or studying in over-crowded cities offer an innovative, inexpensive and effective use of materials and techniques.

Sustainability

Natural materials

A sustainable approach to construction includes the use of locally sourced, natural materials that can be easily replenished (for example, using reed for roof thatching).

Green structures

A green roof or wall is one that uses sedum matting and low-growing, drought-resistant plants. The plants are placed on a drained base that is affixed to a growing mat, and the mat then is attached to a roof or wall structure. Incorporating a 'green' roof or walls in design schemes provides impact to the architecture's aesthetic and will also contribute to a cleaner urban environment.

Orientation

The most considered architectural designs use aspects of site orientation to capitalise on natural lighting, solar power and passive heat gain to ensure that the building naturally warms up and that heat is dissipated through it over the course of the day.

New uses for old materials

Recycling materials is now an important consideration. It is possible to create contemporary architecture that incorporates reconstituted, reclaimed or reused materials, from steel frameworks to brick walls.

Energy efficiency

Architects should consider the way in which their building design may source, harness, consume and conserve energy. Ideally, buildings should source and harness renewable energy and consume and conserve energy as efficiently as possible.

Traditional techniques

Using locally sourced materials and traditional construction techniques offers an effective and sustainable approach to architecture.

Local infrastructure

The infrastructures (such as transport systems and local amenities) that surround a building may also contribute towards its potential to be a sustainable architecture.

Smart materials

The properties of smart materials alter in response to changes in external stimuli. For example, they may alter their shape or colour in response to changes in temperature or exposure to light.

Light-emitting materials

When stimulated electronically these materials can emit different coloured lights, which are preprogrammed to respond to sound or other criteria.

Shape-memory materials

Shape-memory materials can change shape and then reconfigure back to their original form.

Virtual reality

CAD technology can produce realistic impressions of an unrealised architecture. This means that virtual spaces can be created, understood, explored and evaluated before being developed as real environments.

Biomimetic materials

These materials are developed for use in buildings, but mimic aspects of organic or plant life. An example might be a material that changes colour (as a chameleon might) to adapt to its surrounding environment.

Living structures

Living structures offer both an innovative and sustainable future building option. For example, a 'living wall' is multi-layered: as well as providing the usual functions (such as bearing the load of the structure), one of its layers will be able to support vegetation and plant life; this means that the structure can 'live' and grow over time.

Nano materials

These man-made materials exist at a microscopic scale and are engineered to change in response to certain situations. For example, a wall could appear to reflect light through the use of thousands of embedded electrical circuits.

Project: Ray and Maria Stata Center
Location: MIT, Massachusetts, USA
Architect: Frank Gehry
Date: 2004

The Ray and Maria Stata Center's variegated façades of brick, painted aluminium, and stainless steel are Gehry's own brand of contextual design.

In architecture, innovation in material use tends to stem from the migration and adaptation of application in other industries (such as aircraft construction or space travel). Some of the earliest innovations in architectural material application came from unrelated areas. In the early 20th century, for example, a laminated, plastic sheet material called Formica was invented. Now widely used in interior applications, Formica had originally been conceived as an electrical insulator. Innovation in the architectural application of materials is often the result of lateral thinking.

In architecture, innovation can describe advances in the properties of materials and the functionality that this can provide the architect. It can also describe the inventive and ingenious ways in which these new materials are used. To find new methods of material function and application, a creative approach is often necessary. Architects and designers need to discover innovative possibilities through experimentation.

Interdisciplinary

The appropriation of scientific and technological advances can also inform architectural innovation. One such example can be found in the advances made in telecommunications technologies, which have produced a new family of touch-sensitive materials.

For example, screens originally designed for computers and mobile phones are now being specified in architectural designs to create interactive walls and bespoke networking systems. Advances in telecommunications technologies have also allowed the architect to create spaces that can be controlled remotely; devices and systems can be activated (or deactivated) via a mobile phone and this is affecting the way we use our buildings. Perhaps Le Corbusier's vision of a home as a machine for living has advanced a step further.

Reinvention and reinterpretation

In this context, architectural innovation is not just limited to advances in material science and the application of increasingly sophisticated materials. The term can also describe the use of a known material in a new or different way. For example, glass is now being used in architecture in previously unimaginable ways. Historically, it was not used structurally due to its fragility. Today, the use of laminated layers using tempered or toughened glass has increased the potential of the material and allowed it to serve a load-bearing function. Similarly, glass tubes provide a stable structural form and so can be used to realise glass skeleton buildings.

Innovative forms

Innovation can also be evident in architectural forms. Should the architect choose to do so, buildings can now assume incredibly fluid and dynamic forms. The specification of certain materials may (inaccurately) indicate a certain structural form, but traditional materials such as concrete and steel can be used in increasingly innovative ways and so allow buildings to be sculptural and almost organic in shape. Architects such as Frank Gehry and Zaha Hadid use their understanding of materials to achieve innovative forms. Gehry's architecture is often clad with titanium plates that serve almost as a form of armour covering the steel-frame structure underneath, offering the opportunity to produce structures that have even greater impact.

Innovative forms are also seen in those buildings that easily adapt to suit the changing needs of their users. For example, interior spaces that can be reconfigured to accommodate different functions and demands such as a family-friendly space, a home-working area or the needs of a disabled user. Such designs display the architect's innovative conceptual thinking, as well as an innovative realised form. To produce an environment that is adaptable is also a sustainable solution to architecture.

Architectural design should have the capacity for reuse when it has fulfilled its intended function; in doing so, future needs are being considered, possibly the most innovative aspect of architectural design.

Project: Universiteitsbibliotheek
Location: Utrecht, The Netherlands
Architect: Wiel Arets
Dates: 2001–2004

Dutch architect Wiel Arets used concrete in a new way in his library design for the University of Utrecht. Described as 'an elegant box' the library's façade consists of printed glass alternating with black texturised concrete. The glass face has an image of bamboo trees printed on it, which filters the incoming light. The texturised concrete panels add a sense of relief to an otherwise flat wall, creating texture and depth. Arets' design uses concrete and glass in new ways, exploring surface changes that can be made to both materials.

Sustainability has become a necessary consideration in architecture. For the architect, this consideration starts with the conceptual thinking and continues to be at the forefront throughout the design process. Factors such as how the building will respond to its site, the efficiency of its energy-harnessing and consumption, the material specification for the building's construction, the construction techniques and more many more will affect how sustainable a building is.

As well as the sustainability of the design and construction, the sustainability of the building's operation is another key consideration. Where possible, buildings should be carefully designed so that they respond to local climate conditions, use renewable energy resources and are well insulated so that they operate using as little additional energy as possible.

Recycling and reuse

The most sustainable way to build is to reduce the quantity of raw materials used, so specifying the use of recycled materials in a build is a sound option. Recycled glass, steel and concrete all offer the architect viable alternatives to the consumption of raw materials, and innovation in material application can also offer yet more sustainable options. Japanese architect Shigeru Ban, for example, has designed a gridshell structure using cardboard tubes for the structural support.

Using reclaimed materials will also contribute to a sustainable architecture. Perhaps a long-term, sustainable approach can be achieved if we begin to think of the materials we use as component parts that, once used in one structure, can be dismantled (once the structure has served its purpose) and reused in other building schemes.

The need to consider the source of our building materials has become increasingly important. There is a growing demand for materials to be sourced close to their site (in order to reduce the fuel use in transportation). This demand inadvertently echoes the most fundamental requirement of all architecture: to create shelter using materials that come from the locality, which historically created an architecture that was of the place it came from.

Sustainable resources

Key to sustainable architecture is that the building materials themselves are, as far as is possible, sustainable. Using timber from sustainable forests is one often-cited example, another is straw, which has been used in construction for centuries. Straw offers a high quality of insulation, can be treated with fire retardant to make it less flammable and plastered or rendered to make it waterproof. Reed and other materials have also been used for thatch roofing.

The basic components of materials such as biopolymers and biodegradable plastics are derived from natural, renewable materials. All of these, and more, present the architect with functional, efficient and viable alternatives to the use of non-renewable materials.

Green walls and roofs

The demand for more sustainable environments has fuelled an innovative application of materials and technology that is changing the way our cities look. An example of this is the concept of 'green' walls and roofs. These are vegetated layers that sit on top of the conventional roof or wall surfaces of a building. Roof and wall surfaces have previously been considered as 'hard' however, the green option presents the possibility of incorporating living, growing and textured roofs and walls in buildings, creating a new architectural aesthetic and a new ecological habitat for the city.

There are ideas to extend the concept of green walls or roofs. By applying the same principle of structural vegetation to a tower block or skyscraper form, it is argued that a 'vertical farm' can be created and used as an indoor growing environment in the city. The crops can be grown all year round using a fraction of land space for cultivation. Similarly, the concept of the 'living skyscraper' describes a residential micro-environment that can offer the necessary functionality for the occupants to grow their own food and harness their own energy – a sort of urban form of self-sufficiency.

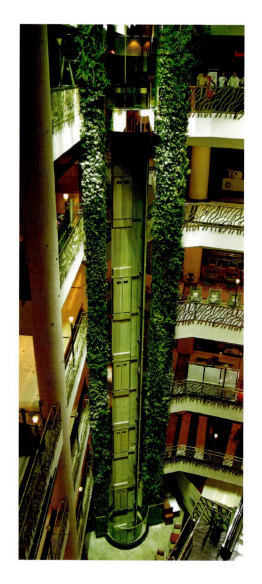

Projects: Hôtel du Département (left),
Emporium Shopping Mall (right)
Locations: Hauts-du-Seine, France
(left)**, Bangkok, Thailand** (right)
Architect: Patrick Blanc
Dates: 2005 (both projects)

Patrick Blanc's Vertical Gardens are
living installations. The lush wall
plantings, which are often several
storeys tall, require no soil and come
equipped with a self-sufficient watering
system. Using a system that allows
plants to grow without any soil
allows for natural living beauty in
otherwise arid places, producing
dynamic, growing building façades.

The future of material application in buildings is exciting. Architects have at their disposal a range of hi-tech, intelligent and enhanced materials that are responsive to all sorts of conditions. Materials are crossing from one area of industrial use to another: a material used in space technology today, for example, may be tomorrow's super-insulating material for the home.

The future for materials in architecture includes innovation in material application and consideration of virtual materials and environments. Virtual environments allow all sorts of possibilities to be considered in terms of construction, materiality and form. CAD environments are becoming more and more sophisticated and allow simulation of rooms, buildings and complete environments to be virtually tested before they become real.

Prefabrication

Prefabrication is an important aspect of construction today and will continue to be so in the future. Techniques previously used in furniture and product manufacture are now commonly used to realise building designs. This has required a conceptual shift from the perspective of considering a building as an object to thinking of it as a machine that is created from pre-cut, ready-to-assemble component parts.

The key advantages of prefabricated building designs is the predictability (and reliability) of the construction and site time they offer and that it is possible for the architect to control the quality of the pieces as they are manufactured and assembled in a factory (disadvantages may include the transportation required to get the pieces to site and the size of the component parts).

Prefabricated architecture has an important place in current and future construction systems. Prefabricated pieces can be quickly assembled and dismantled, so as well as offering solutions to current architectural problems they have the potential for future reuse in different locations or projects.

Smart materials

A smart material is one that is not static, and through technological support (such as motors or sensors) it can react to changing environments and respond to them accordingly. These materials are highly engineered, changing colour, reacting to temperature changes or even altering their shape in order to adapt to their surrounding environment.

In the context of architectural application the specification of smart materials could include photochromic windows. These change from transparent to a colour when exposed to light, and revert to transparency when the light is dimmed or blocked. Another example could be the incorporation of photovoltaic materials, which transform energy from one source to another and are often used for solar cells or panels.

Other examples include biomimetic materials, which are designed to mimic aspects of natural organisms. So a plant's ability to collect water or filter sunlight can be translated into buildings through biomimetic materials that are developed and specifically engineered to mimic the same function. Microscopic nanomaterials are man-made and engineered to respond to specific situations; for example, a wall could appear to reflect light through the use of thousands of embedded electrical circuits.

To use smart materials in buildings effectively we need to understand the properties and capabilities of the material rather than the aesthetic they provide. When conventional materials are used in a building they will have a fixed appearance (although they may age and slightly change colour), but smart materials need to be considered in an ever-changing environment.

Using smart materials can produce an architecture that is fluid and responsive to changing conditions. The designer needs to understand the enormous potential for the application of these materials and experiment with them to develop a new paradigm for architecture.

Project: The Royal Observatory
Location: Greenwich, London, UK
Architects: Allies and Morrison
Date: 2007

Allies and Morrison were commissioned to restore the existing South Building at the Royal Observatory in Grenwich and to create a new structure to house a planetarium. The 118-seat planetarium is set within a distinctive truncated cone structure, which is made from concrete and clad in a carapace of pre-patinated phosphor bronze. The exacting geometric form required precise construction. The tilted cone aligns with the North Star and the glass roof is parallel with the equator, thus reflecting the northern hemisphere of the night sky.

This book serves as a starting point in the exploration of material application in architecture. It has also begun to unravel architecture into its constituent parts and emphasise that the materiality of a building is everything. It creates the form, structure and texture of a space, and affects light, temperature and a user's entire experience of the architecture. To reinforce this, an understanding of construction techniques and how material components come together to 'make' a building is invaluable.

New building materials are being introduced to the marketplace all the time and it is the architect's responsibility to be aware of them and understand their potential so that we can continue to expand the possibilities of their application. I hope that the case studies presented here have demonstrated the many ways in which architects can create inspirational environments through their interpretation and application of construction and materials.

All designers have a responsibility to consider the use of materials so that those specified for a new build or the refurbishment of an existing one are carefully chosen from sustainable sources, and that this is matched by an equally careful consideration of the way in which they are applied to the architecture.

It is important to establish what materials and techniques are available and the potential of these within the context of a design. Beyond this, however, the key to great application of materials in architecture is to be inventive – remember the only 'real' creative limits are the boundaries of your imagination.

**Project: Burraworrin House
Location: Melbourne, Australia
Architect: Gregory Burgess Architects**

Burraworrin ('Magpie') House, on the coastline of the Mornington Peninsula, houses three generations of one family. It is a building which celebrates and supports the activities that occur in the home. The exterior is clad in Victorian hardwood stringy bark and the building's parabolic curves, projecting roof lines and bow-shaped hulls, are clad in radially sawn timber.

Construction + materiality

Stone

Limestone

Marble

Dressed stone

Stone wall cladding

Slate wall cladding

Grey granite

Brick

Running bond

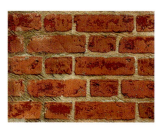

Flemish bond

Stretcher bond

Dry stone wall

Rubble stone wall

Roman brick wall

Construction + materiality

Concrete

Concrete block

Light-emitting concrete

Surface-treated concrete

Polished concrete

Transferred-surface concrete

Coloured concrete

Timber

Red Beech

Douglas Fir

European Oak

European Beech

Maple

Cork

Samples panel

Glass

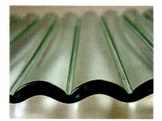

Cast glass

Fused glass

Coloured glass

Foam glass

Glass fin

Glass fibre

Steel

Stainless steel

Steel fabric

Perforated steel

Steel cable

Weathered steel

Steel frame

Construction + materiality

Innovative materials

Translucent concrete

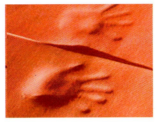

Shock-absorbing foam

LED mesh

Ceramic foam

Concrete fabric

Optical fibres

Composite materials

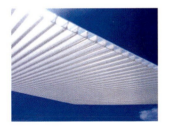

Corrugated plastic

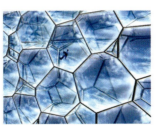

Ethylene tetrafluoroethylene (ETFE)

Moulded plastic

Rubber flooring

Titanium cladding

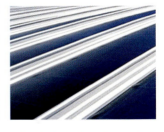

Kalzip AluPlusSolar solar panels

Samples panel

Alloys
A term that is used to describe the combination of metal with at least one other element. An alloy is stronger than its constituent metal. Most engineering applications for metals are alloys.

Biopolymer
A polymer is a molecule made of many parts. While the term 'polymer' (in popular usage) is often used to describe plastic, the term actually refers to a large class of natural and synthetic materials with a variety of properties and functions. A biopolymer is a class of polymers made from natural rather than synthetic materials.

Cladding
This refers to the covering or overlaying of one material with another. In architectural terms it refers to the outer layer of a building. Cladding needs to be weatherproof and will provide a building with its 'skin'.

Composite material
A material that is composed of several different raw ingredients. The composition of other base materials can create a new product that combines properties of the original sources.

Ethylene tetrafluoroethylene (ETFE)
Famously used to create the biomes at the Eden Project in Cornwall, ETFE is a lightweight plastic that can be moulded to create many shapes. It is semi-opaque and is often used in roof applications.

Fabric
A building's fabric refers to the architectural form and structure.

Green roof
A roof of a building that is partially or completely covered with vegetation and soil. The soil and vegetation is planted over a waterproofing membrane. A green roof will not only accommodate plants, but will also provide a habitat for wildlife.

Green wall
Much like a green roof, a green wall is a wall that contains a purpose-designed irrigation system. It has within it a variety of plant species and with careful maintenance creates a living environment. A green wall can feature either on the inside or outside of a building.

Hybrid
A material that combines several other materials is described as hybrid. A hybrid is a new derivative from several other material sources.

Mechanical properties
Refers to characteristics of materials that are usually measured through changing or destroying the material, such as strength, hardness, elasticity.

Membrane
A membrane is a skin that is used to separate one area from another. Most frequently a membrane is used to separate wet spaces from dry ones.

Permeable
A material that allows water or air to pass through it can be described as permeable. The permeability of the material is the measurement of this movement through it.

Photochromic materials
A photochromic material is one that changes colour when exposed to light or ultraviolet radiation. In architectural terms, this may be a surface coating on a wall or window and is usually applied to alter a building's façade.

Physical properties
Compared to mechanical properties, physical properties can be measured without destroying or changing the material.

Polytetrafluoroethylene (PTFE)
PTFE is a manufactured material that is commonly used as a coating on textiles to make them more durable and waterproof. In architecture, PTFE is most often used for roof applications, as is the case in the example of the O2 Arena in London.

Photovoltaic materials
Photovoltaic materials generate voltage when they are exposed to visible and invisible light. These materials usually take the form of solar panels or screens that are carefully organised and positioned to best absorb sunlight.

Reclaimed
Materials that are taken from an existing building (for example, bricks or tiles) and incorporated into a new project can be described as reclaimed. Reclaiming materials is an architectural form of recycling, appropriating their use from one context to another.

Renewable
This term can be applied to those energy or material sources that are easily replenished by natural processes at a rate comparable or faster than their rate of consumption. Example of renewable energy sources include sunlight or wind power and renewable materials include those made from wood or plant fibre.

Smart material
Smart materials are those that respond to stimuli such as light, temperature and electrical field by changing their form, colour or viscosity, etc. An example of a smart material in an architectural application might be wallpaper that changes its colour or pattern depending on the levels of light or different temperatures that it is exposed to.

Sustainable
If a material is sustainable, then its production is capable of being continued with minimal long-term effect on the environment.

Synthetic
A synthetic material is one that is man-made and engineered from carefully selected components that suit a particular functional requirement. Some of these components may be organic and others derived form other synthetic sources.

Tensile strength
A measure of the amount of stress a material is able to withstand when it is stretched.

Translucent
A material that allows light to pass through it can be described as translucent. For example, glass is a translucent material commonly used in architecture and construction.

Construction + materiality

Page 3: courtesy and copyright of David Lambert and Nissen Adams Architects

Page 6: courtesy and copyright of Nigel Young / Foster + Partners

Page 12: courtesy and copyright of RIBA Library Photographs Collection

Page 21: courtesy and copyright of Stanton Williams Architects and Peter Cook

Pages 32–35: all photographs courtesy and copyright of Hélène Binet

Page 33: courtesy of Jonathan Woolf Architects

Pages 36–39: all photographs courtesy and copyright of Hélène Binet

Page 37: courtesy of Eric Parry Architects

Page 41: courtesy and copyright of Roland Halbe/RIBA Library Photographs Collection

Page 44: courtesy and copyright of RIBA Library Photographs Collection

Page 47: courtesy and copyright of RIBA Library Photographs Collection

Page 48 and 51: courtesy and copyright of The Concrete Centre

Page 53: courtesy and copyright of David Lambert and Nissen Adams Architects

Page 55: courtesy and copyright of Liao Yusheng

Pages 57–58: courtesy and copyright of Liao Yusheng

Page 59: courtesy and copyright of Martin Pearce

Pages 60–63: courtesy and copyright of Hélène Binet and Zaha Hadid Architects

Page 64: courtesy and copyright of Reinhard Görner

Pages 66–67: courtesy and copyright of Werner Hutmacher

Page 68: courtesy and copyright of Sean Godsell

Page 73: courtesy and copyright of NTPL/Derek Croucher

Page 77: courtesy and copyright of Robin Baker Architects

Pages 78–79: courtesy and copyright of Studio KAP and Keith Hunter

Page 80: courtesy and copyright of Studio KAP and Kenneth Bane

Pages 85–89: all photographs courtesy and copyright of Edward Cullinan Architects; photographers: Gareth Mantle and Keegan Duigenan

Pages 90–93: all photographs courtesy and copyright of Sean Godsell

Pages 94–97: all photographs courtesy and copyright of Glen Howells Architects; photographer: Warwick Sweeney

Page 103: courtesy and copyright of Bernard Cox/RIBA Library Photographs Collection

Page 104: courtesy and copyright of Danielle Tinero/RIBA Library Photographs Collection

Page 110: courtesy and copyright of Vinesh Pomal

Page 114: courtesy and copyright of Martin Pearce

Pages 118–121: all photographs courtesy and copyright of Nigel Young / Foster + Partners

Pages 122–124: all photographs courtesy and copyright of Grimshaw Architects

Page 127: courtesy and copyright of dRMM, Alex de Rijke/ Jonas Lencer/ Michael Mack/ Philip Marsh/ Satoshi Isono/ Mirko Immendoerfer

Pages 139–141: all photographs courtesy and copyright of Liao Yusheng

Page 142: courtesy and copyright of Colin Tomsett

Pages 144–147 courtesy and copyright of Stanton Williams Architects

Page 148–151: all photographs courtesy and copyright of dRMM

Pages 162–163: photographs courtesy and copyright of Patrick Blanc

Pages 166–167: drawing courtesy and copyright of Allies and Morrison; photograph courtesy Dennis Gilbert and copyright of the National Maritime Museum

Page 168: courtesy and copyright of Trevor Mein and Gregory Burgess Architects

Glossary and picture credits

This book has benefited enormously from the input of teaching colleagues, practising architects and students alike.

I would like to thank all those architects, design practices and individual contributors who have supplied images, specification details, supplementary information and found the time and desire to support the process of compiling this book.

Special thanks are due to Nicki Crowson, who researched a number of topics in the book and provided a range of reference and resource material. Thanks are also due to Colin Tomsett and Andrea Verenini who helped with the book's research.

Finally thank you to Brian Morris and Caroline Walmsley at AVA Publishing, who have cajoled, encouraged and edited, and to Jane Harper for the book's wonderful design.